OVERNIGHT
ENTREPRENEURS

OVERNIGHT ENTREPRENEURS
UNUSUAL START, OUTSTANDING JOURNEY!

BHANU AIYER

Notion Press

Old No. 38, New No. 6
McNichols Road, Chetpet
Chennai - 600 031

First Published by Notion Press 2017
Copyright © Bhanu Aiyer 2017
All Rights Reserved.

ISBN 978-1-946641-01-4

This book has been published with all reasonable efforts taken to make the material error-free after the consent of the author. No part of this book shall be used, reproduced in any manner whatsoever without written permission from the author, except in the case of brief quotations embodied in critical articles and reviews.

The Author of this book is solely responsible and liable for its content including but not limited to the views, representations, descriptions, statements, information, opinions and references ["Content"]. The Content of this book shall not constitute or be construed or deemed to reflect the opinion or expression of the Publisher or Editor. Neither the Publisher nor Editor endorse or approve the Content of this book or guarantee the reliability, accuracy or completeness of the Content published herein and do not make any representations or warranties of any kind, express or implied, including but not limited to the implied warranties of merchantability, fitness for a particular purpose. The Publisher and Editor shall not be liable whatsoever for any errors, omissions, whether such errors or omissions result from negligence, accident, or any other cause or claims for loss or damages of any kind, including without limitation, indirect or consequential loss or damage arising out of use, inability to use, or about the reliability, accuracy or sufficiency of the information contained in this book.

CONTENTS

Prelude	*vii*
Preface	*xi*
Acknowledgments	*xiii*
1. Growing Up	1
2. Tumbling Down	28
3. Setting Foot	52
4. Climbing the Ladder	67
5. Finding Love	79
6. The Beginning of an Adventure	96
7. Becoming Smarter	121
8. Spanning Wings	135
9. Getting Rewarded	144
Epilogue	*147*

PRELUDE

Sarayu was sleeping in the recliner, a lovely smile frozen on her face. She must have been dreaming about the baby, about yet another pink frock, yet another toy and yet another book she was planning to buy for the baby.

She heard a familiar voice coming from far away. The voice grew louder as its owner, her mother, came closer. A splash of cold water hit her face. Now the voice had grown to a deafening decibel level, hurling despicable abuses at her.

Sara's breathing became rapid. Her eyebrows furrowed. Lips quivered. She tried to scream but her vocal cords refused to cooperate. She tried to run away but not a muscle in her body would move. She was staring at the beautiful yet terrifying face in front of her. She could not bear the abuses that came streaming from those beautiful pink lips. She was transfixed and terrorized. She wished that the verbal abuses would stop. The top of her head was in splitting pain owing to a blow delivered by her mother's clinched fist. Tears were rolling down her cheeks uncontrollably. She started to sob.

Suddenly, the abuses stopped. Her mother raised her left leg to kick her in the stomach. "No…! My baby…!" she screamed as she placed her hands protectively over her belly.

"Sara! Wake up. What's the matter, girl?" her husband was patting her cheeks gently. She woke up and looked at him. He was leaning over her, wiping her tears gently. She was drenched thoroughly in sweat. Her body was trembling. He made her sit up, cuddled her gently in his arms and kissed softly on her forehead. His concerned voice and warm hug brought her to reality.

"Nothing. Just one of those nightmares." She gave him an assuring smile. "I am alright."

"Another nightmare! But, it's been so long, may be a year since you stopped having these nightmares. What's the matter now? Were you thinking of past incidents? I have told you many times not to think of your mother," he reproached her.

She too wondered what brought back that particular nightmare. Then she realized that she had actually slept for half-an-hour at a stretch. She had hardly been able to sleep for ten minutes over the past few months. The baby had been very active ever since it first kicked. How did she sleep for so long? Oh god! Oh god!

"The baby is not moving!" she gasped. He panicked and called the obstetrician.

"Don't worry, dear. I was expecting the baby to arrive before you were full-term. Check-in at the hospital at the earliest. I will be there in twenty minutes. Do not panic. Everything will be fine. It's almost thirty-two weeks. I will ask the hospital to prepare the theatre for a caesarean section," the motherly doctor assured.

'Hey honey! Want to see mom so soon? Hold on there, baby. Just a few more hours. You will see your mom and dad.

Honey! You know what? Your mother is the best mother in the world. Yes, she will be the best mother in the world because she knows exactly how a mother should not be.' The baby gave a kick as if it understood.

"Come on Sara. Let's go. The cab is waiting outside." She checked the gas valve, switched off the lights and fans, said a quick prayer in front of Pillayar (the Hindu god with the head of an elephant) and they left the house.

PREFACE

What are the ingredients to produce successful entrepreneurs?

Qualification, Business *gyan*, Experience in the field, Sizable investment...

I am sure these points came to your mind when you read that question.

But, what if I say, we - my partner and I did not have any of the above when we plunged into entrepreneurship at the age of twenty-two? And, if I go on to add that we have been successful for the past twenty-six years and are still going strong?

No, this is no 'rags-to-riches-overnight' fairy tale. It is a journey that started quite humbly and was unplanned. We stumbled many times and picked ourselves up every time. The very unfortunate circumstances that befell us acted as springboards for serendipity.

The only ingredients we had were determination, hard work, perseverance, unwavering goals and the trust we had in ourselves. It was as simple as that.

If we, who started as the most unlikely entrepreneurs, can succeed then anybody can. Especially those who have one or more of the ingredients listed above.

I wanted to share the thrilling experience of our roller coaster ride, hence this book.

ACKNOWLEDGMENTS

This book is the fruition of my authorship. I fondly acknowledge and thank those who helped me bear this fruit:

The expert gardeners who helped the raw fruit ripen: the Notion Press team; the editing team for polishing my raw manuscript into a gleaming novel and the design team for all those patient reproductions until we arrived at the best cover design.

My mentor who put the right kind and amount of fertilizer and fenced the garden against potential threats like self-doubt: Kiruba Shankar. And a special thanks to his caring parents who provided the growing tree with extra nutrients.

My fellow trees in the beautiful garden who provided the much needed camaraderie to survive cyclones and sandstorms: my author buddies; Abinav, Amreen Makhani, Sangeeta Shankaran Sumesh, Sathya Narayanan, Shambavi, Srividhya Vaidyanathan, and others.

My friends who watered the small plant and helped it grow into a fruit-bearing tree: Sridharan Ranganathan, Mahalakshmi Krishna Kumar, Dr. Anbazhahan Rajaram and Senith Mathews.

The Good Samaritans who planted the sapling in the right garden at the right time and made sure that it grew: my cousin, Radha Suresh and my friend, Padmanabhan Ravindran.

The sunlight which helped the seed sprout: my son Anirudh.

The soil in which the seed germinated; without the support of which the tree could not stand for even a second: my husband Murugan.

And finally, the one who sowed the seed and gave it the potency to thrive against all odds: my late father Shri. Chandramouli Aiyer.

Chapter 1

GROWING UP

It was a pleasant morning in the middle of August 1984.

Sarayu got down from the bus at the 'polytechnic' bus stop. Many students alighted with her. They entered the college campus through a small gate. The campus looked huge. The big trees and grand buildings could be seen from the road. The air was cool and the breeze carried the sweet smell of flowers. There was a hillock across the road, opposite the gate. It was a small, rocky hillock with a big shady tree at the top. The tree bore bright yellow flowers. Sarayu fell in love with the place at once.

She looked around and saw one girl standing and staring at the small entrance. 'She must be a fresher too.' She smiled at the other girl who was equally clueless about where to go. When Sarayu came to the college with her father for all her admission formalities, they had come through the main entrance.

"Are you a fresher?" Sara asked her. The other girl nodded. "Me too. Come, let's go in together," Sara smiled at her. "My name is Sarayu. Sara for short."

"I am Jaya," the other girl replied.

The campus was huge with majestic trees, manicured gardens, beautiful shrubs and vibrant flowers everywhere. As they walked towards a big building which looked like the administrative office, a group of six or seven boys, who looked big enough to be called men, walked towards them. From a distance, Sara noticed that the boys were joking about the two of them and laughing.

Sarayu was short; she was just a couple of inches short of five feet and she was thin. She looked like a cut-out made of slightly thick cardboard. At sixteen, she looked like a thirteen-year-old. Jaya was tall and hefty. She was six feet in height and two feet in width. At sixteen, she looked like a twenty-year-old. The sight of the two of them walking together obviously amused the boys.

One of the boys, who looked like the leader of the gang, looked at Jaya and asked, "Are you freshers?"

"Yes," Sara replied. "Which way do we go for the auditorium?"

The boys laughed again. "Which way do you go? I will tell you," the leader grinned, "but before that you need to recite A,B,C,D to me."

"A,B,C,D," said Sara.

"No, not like that. You need to recite it from A to Z and do a sit-up as you say each letter."

"No," Sara said firmly.

"What?" he did not expect this.

"NO. I won't do it," Sara said firmly as she held her head high and stared right into the boy's eyes.

The boy was not sure how to take it any further. He was very disappointed and angry. "You don't know who I am," he shook his index finger almost like he was warning her. "I will let you go now. But, I will deal with your cheekiness later." He was clearly frustrated.

Jaya was already trembling and dragged Sara away before she could retort. After they walked about fifty meters, they heard the boys laughing loudly behind them.

When Sara and Jaya were about to enter the building, the same group passed by them. They walked very close to them and strangely they were all very silent. No talking, no laughing. Suddenly, Sara felt something crawling down the back of her neck. She quickly reached back and fished it out, 'What is it?'

She gasped as she looked at the object in her fist. It was a big cockroach. Disgusted, she threw the cockroach away. It flew into a nearby bush and disappeared. By then, the boys had turned and were looking at her; they expected an amusing scene to unfold before them.

She quickly regained her composure, let out a forced laugh and continued walking. She shot a cheeky look at the gang leader as she walked past them. Meanwhile, Sara did not know when exactly, but Jaya had fled the scene. Amused by her timidity, she chuckled.

She reached the big auditorium. It was four times bigger than her school auditorium. A staff member was handing out pamphlets to the new students as they entered the auditorium. It gave details such as the layout of the campus, guidelines to be followed, a list of apparatus and books to be bought by first-year students, dress code for the labs and other general campus dos and don'ts.

There was a stage with two podiums on either side. A mic was on the podium on the left. The stage was about three feet above the floor, with steps on either side to the top. Five chairs were placed on the stage.

The hall was divided into two portions. On one side, there were 180 freshers, all aged between fifteen and seventeen. The other half had been divided into three sections, each with four rows of chairs. The decibel level of the energetic crowd was so high that the noise reached the classrooms where the seniors were attending classes.

Students were introducing themselves to each other. The first question every student seemed to ask the other after introduction was, "What marks did you score in tenth grade?" Whenever the questions was asked and answered between any two people, one could guess even from a distance who had scored more among the two; the neck of the person with the higher score would grow an inch taller.

It was the Government Polytechnic College in Vellore. Vellore is neither big enough to be called a city nor small enough to be called a town. It is a big town. It is the capital of the North Arcot district in the state of Tamil Nadu in southern India.

The state-government-run institute was one of the most sought-after institutes, offering three-year diploma courses in engineering. Unlike engineering colleges that offered four-year degree courses which required a twelfth grade pass for admission, these polytechnic colleges admitted students after their tenth grade. In the eighties and nineties, one needed to score very high marks to get admission in a polytechnic college.

In those days, after the tenth grade, children from affluent and upper-middle class families preferred to take up eleventh and twelfth then seek admission in engineering colleges which offered degrees; the duration of the course would be four years. Those from middle class and lower-middle class families preferred these polytechnic colleges which offered diplomas for the duration of three years.

The diploma holders with high scores could join a degree course. After getting the diploma, they could pursue a degree, they could start working or they could do both simultaneously by working at a full-time job and joining a part-time degree course. The attractive multiple options it presented for their future got so many students to apply to polytechnic colleges that only the top students, the ones who scored more than four hundred out of five hundred marks in their tenth grade exams, could get admission to these institutions.

Suddenly the high-volume cacophony receded to a low-volume murmur. Everyone's attention was drawn to the entrance near the stage. Five important looking, middle-aged gentlemen were entering through the doorway. They went onstage and occupied the chairs there. Now the crowd was absolutely quiet.

One of the gentlemen, who looked to be more important than the others, stood up and walked to the podium. He was tall and hefty. He wore a sandal-colored Safari suit. His salt and pepper hair gave him a respectable look to his face.

"Good morning students. I am the Principal of this esteemed institution, which will celebrate its silver jubilee this year. I welcome you all to this college on behalf of the Vice Principal, my fellow professors, lecturers, and the other staff of this college," said the Principal.

"I am going to call your names one by one in the order of admission, and I will also announce your section." He took out gold-framed bifocal spectacles from his pocket. One of the staff standing offstage handed him a sheet of paper, probably the list of students, to the Principal. He took the paper and looked at the students with a friendly smile.

"There are three sections of sixty students each. When I announce your name and section, please move to the columns marked here — A, B and C."

Then another staff member removed the barricade chain hung across the length of the hall.

The Principal continued, "First year lessons will be common to all three sections. Next year, you will be sent to one of the three departments we have – mechanical, civil and, electrical and electronics – sixty students for each department. That will be according to your preference and *also*," he stressed on 'also', paused for a second, and continued dramatically, "your performance in your first year. So, you better do well in the first year to be considered for your choice of department." He looked around to ensure that the candidates understood the importance of their 'performance' in their first year. "Now, I will read the list."

Growing Up

"Sarayu," he looked up from his list. Sara stood up. "435 marks out of 500 in the tenth grade." The gentlemen on the stage started clapping and the crowd in the hall followed suit.

The Principal went on, "The college welcomes our first female student. As you all know, this twenty-five-year-old institute has been a boys' college so far. We will be a co-education institute from this year. Sarayu, please go to A section."

Sarayu walked to the section marked A with a proud gait, almost like the Principal had placed the crown of England on her head. She enjoyed the limelight she received. She occupied a chair in the front row of the section.

The Principal continued, "Ravi, another 435 out of 500; section B," There was another round of applause for the boy. Sara felt as if someone had snatched her crown. Her elevated head returned to its usual altitude. She gave the boy a sheepish smile as he passed her and took his seat in section B. He returned a sweet smile.

The Principal continued reading down the list for about twenty entries and then the other gentlemen took turns to read the list, and the candidates continued occupying the sections.

Hariharan was a lanky lad with a shy demeanor. His oily hair, loose attire and flip-flops made it obvious that he was from a small town. He was from Thiruvannamalai, a small town about eighty-six kilometers from Vellore. His father was a middle-level manager in a state-government owned warehouse there. His mother was a housewife. He had an elder sister and two younger brothers. Their house had one hall and a kitchen next to it; there was no door between the two. The hall was the family's living room during the day and their bedroom at night.

They had a garden at the back of the house. There was a bathroom and a toilet on one side of the garden. There was a well on the other side with a circular cement platform surrounding it. They used to wash the vessels there. There was a rectangular stone fixed by the platform. It was used to wash clothes. They had to draw water from the well for drinking, cooking, bathing, and washing.

Hari's father was a hard-working person. He used to procure things for the family from sources which offered the cheapest and best solutions. He used to grow vegetables and fruit-bearing trees in the garden. The garden took care of half of the family's nourishment needs.

Hari's mother was a kind, soft-spoken woman. Though she had studied only in elementary school she possessed good general knowledge and common sense. She was a very good cook. She managed to provide the children with simple but healthy food within her husband's meagre income.

Hari's father was a strict person. He did not like the kids wasting time in play and other entertainment; he wanted them to spend more time studying. He firmly believed that only good education would uplift the children's lifestyle. He had lost his father at a very tender age and struggled hard to complete his schooling.

He used to work in a brick kiln after school to buy text books. Somehow, with much difficulty, he completed his high school education and joined a government job at a low position with a paltry salary. He wanted his children to achieve better levels of financial security in life. 'Education is the only key; the children cannot afford to waste time on playing and entertainment.' They had three things to do — first study, second study and the third ...yes...study.

Hari's mother was a more practical person. She would let the children play after school, without the knowledge of their father, of course. They could play as much as they wished but had to return home at the stroke of six, the children followed this religiously since they knew not abiding by this rule would jeopardize their playtime. Some delicious evening snacks would welcome them when they returned. After cleaning up and eating, the five of them – the four children and their mother – would listen to the radio for sometime.

Their father would return from the office only at seven O' clock. At six-forty-five sharp, the radio would be switched off and returned to its place by the window. The children would open their books and start reading aloud.

The cacophony of four children reading aloud at the same time would greet their father when he returned from the office. Not that he ever believed that they had been studying for hours sincerely but he would be satisfied that they feared the system and sat down to study even if it was a few minutes. This study session would continue until nine O' clock. After that another radio session, this time it was approved-by-father and would continue till bed time.

The children were generally responsible kids. All four of them would help their mother cook. By the time they turned fifteen, all the children knew how to cook just by watching and helping her. They used to help their father with the gardening. They drew water from the well in turns. Though they had very little in terms of possessions, they were a happy family.

Textbooks would be handed down from older to younger siblings. The shirts Hari outgrew would be passed on to his younger brothers — Kumar and Sekar.

Hari used to be among the top five students in his class. Though his father knew that he was a brilliant student, he thought that his son would not score 400 marks required to get a polytechnic admission. To be on the safe side, he bought application forms from the Vellore government polytechnic as well as from an ITI (Industrial Training Institute), the next option for engineering. These ITIs offered two-year certificate courses in a specific skill and certified one as an electrician, carpenter, etc.

Hari believed that he would get at least 400 marks and he was embarrassed when his father did not believe in him. He studied intensely during the tenth grade exams. He wanted to prove that his father was wrong.

His father was the happiest person on earth when the results came. Hari topped his school with a whopping 428 marks. He got admission to the Vellore government polytechnic without any difficulty.

Growing Up

The college had a hostel for boys from other towns. His family arranged for Hari to stay in the hostel for the first semester. From the second semester onwards, he would stay at his uncle's, his father's elder brother, house in Vellore. This was to cut the expense of the hostel fees.

His uncle was a single business man. He used to travel on business most of the time. So, it was arranged that Hari would cook his own meals during his stay there.

Hari was in B section in his first year. He became friends with his lab team which comprised of a boy, Mani and two girls, Malu and Nandhini. They worked together in the lab and stayed friendly in other classes too. They helped each other with their studies too. Mani also stayed in the hostel so he and Hari became close friends.

In college, the portions seemed to have increased manifold. They were not only vast but also tough. Some students had finished their twelfth grade and joined the diploma since they did not get admission to an engineering college. Such students found the mathematics in engineering easy. They had finished their basics in the eleventh and twelfth. But the poor sixteen-year-olds who were there just after their tenth were devastated. Many students feared that they would fail this paper.

Sara enjoyed every moment she spent in college. Every other week they had cultural programs and sports meets. She took part in music and essay competitions, and debates and she won prizes. She acted in a play conducted by the senior boys.

The final exams for the first semester commenced before she realized it. The first paper in the exam series was engineering drawing; her favorite subject. She was very good at it and she had the chance to get a full score.

The day before the exam, she prepared for many hours past midnight. The next morning she did not wake up at her usual six O' clock. One reason was that she had prepared for too long during the night. The other reason was that her father was out of town to attend a relative's wedding. He used to wake up all his children by giving their feet and shoulders a gentle massage. He would speak in a sweet and soft voice while cajoling them to wake up.

She slept well beyond six-thirty. A sudden splash of cold water hit her head and shook her out of her dreams wildly. She opened her burning eyes. Her mother stood nearby, shouting abuses at the top of her lungs. Sara took a few seconds to comprehend the situation. She was still lying on the mat, paralysed by the splash of cold water and the stream of verbal abuses. This irked her mother more and she kicked Sara's stomach with all her might.

Sara winced. She knew very well that every minute she lay there, the verbal and physical abuse would get worse. She quickly got up, rolled up her mat, folded her bed sheet, put them in their place, brushed her teeth, washed her face, took the broomstick and started to sweep the floor. After that she had to wash the vessels before getting ready for college and leaving for her exams. It was too late and she left home without eating any breakfast. She reached the bus stop half-walking and half-running. Luckily a half-empty bus came and she got a seat.

She checked if she had taken everything required for the exam. The exam hall ticket, two HB pencils, two 2B pencils, two 2H pencils – all neatly sharpened, a sharpener, a foot-long scale, a small ruler, an eraser…oh no! She forgot to take her mini-drafter. She froze. That was the most important thing for a drawing exam. Without a mini-drafter she wouldn't be able to draw anything. Fixing the mini-drafter on the table and then fixing the drawing sheet was the first ritual one had to do before the exam started.

Before she could think of what to do next, the college bus stop arrived and she got down. She could not go back home and bring the drafter. It was too late for that. She made a quick plan to go to the exam supervisor and ask for help. 'Maybe there are some drafters in the college which they loan to students.'

She was almost crying when she greeted the exam supervisor. Her lips trembled when she told him that she forgot to bring the mini-drafter. She asked him if he could arrange for a mini-drafter for her. But he told her that there was no provision for storing drafters at the college. He was obviously annoyed by her forgetfulness. How could a girl forget to bring her mini-drafter to a drawing exam!

The first bell meant for preparing the drawing tables rang. She watched helplessly as other students began to clean and fix their drafters on their desks. Tears started to roll down her cheeks. When the next bell struck, they would start giving out the question paper. What was she going to do with the question paper? She was standing there not knowing whether to leave the exam hall then or later.

A boy from her class, whose name was Sundar, approached the hall supervisor and told him that he wished to offer his drafter to Sara. The supervisor beckoned to Sara.

"You are very lucky. Sundar has decided to give his mini-drafter to you," he said sarcastically.

She was astonished by this generosity and was hesitant to take the drafter. When she asked why would he offer his drafter to her and what would he do without a drafter, he replied that he had not prepared for the exam well and then thrust the drafter into her hands before he walked out of the exam hall without looking back.

Growing Up

Although she lost around twenty minutes due to the unexpected turn of events, she did so well in the exam that she ended up topping the grade with a score of ninety-eight percent. To her surprise, she took just two marks above the minimum requirement for a pass in mathematics, thanks to Jaisri, her lab-mate. She was good at mathematics and she helped Sara scrape through the exam. Sara had done fairly well in the rest of the papers.

On the day of the results, she met Sundar when the class was going to the lab. She thanked him profusely for his generosity and timely help.

"I never thought that someone would donate his drafter to me in the exam hall. You failed the engineering drawing just because you gave your drafter to me, Sundar. But I keep wondering why would you resort to such a foolish sacrifice," she chided him.

"Honestly, I did not prepare well for the exam. I will write the exam next semester and pass. But I thank god for giving me the opportunity to express my love for you in this way. By this act, if I could get a place in your heart, I will be most blessed."

She was taken aback. She did not expect this at all. Oh my god! How stupid! She did not know whether to be angry with him or pity him for such foolishness.

"Sundar, had I known this was your sentiment when you gave me the drafter, I wouldn't have accepted it. I thought that it was an act of generosity. And of course, it is an act of generosity. Let it stay that way. Please do not tell anyone what you said to me. I would like to be your good friend for ever. Nothing more than a good friend."

Sundar was a tall, dark, handsome boy with bright white eyes and teeth. His face grew even darker when he heard her words. His eyes became red and watery.

"I wish I could repay your debt in some way. Hey, I have an idea. I can teach you drawing and help you score well when you write the exam next semester," Sara said apologetically.

The thought that she did not disown him completely gave him some consolation and he agreed to take tuitions from her before his drawing exam.

"On one condition. The next time you talk to me, it will be as a friend only. I don't want to hear any more of this rubbish. Okay?"

He agreed reluctantly and left the place with his head hanging low.

'Where do these boys get such ideas from? All from the movies, promoting teenage love as a big deal.' Sara felt sorry for Sundar.

Growing Up

Sara preferred to take civil engineering since she was fond of design and drafting. Since she secured the top marks in engg. drawing in both semesters she was assured a place in civil engg.

But her father advised against it. He said that the future was brighter for electronics compared to civil, more so for girls, even more so for puny girls like her.

The state-government owned Electricity Board was recruiting diploma engineers in electrical for sub-stations all over the state. So, all the EEE (electrical and electronics engineering) students were hopeful of getting a placement there. Almost all the first-class diploma engineers from the previous year were recruited by the TNEB (Tamil Nadu Electricity Board). To get a job in TNEB or any big public sector industry, one needed to earn a first-class diploma, which means an average score of sixty percent or more in the final year.

Her father insisted that her physique was not suitable for the harsh-working environment a civil engineer would face. Consequently, she changed her choice to EEE.

Hari decided well before joining college that he would do EEE. There was a tape recorder at home. He used to amplify the output with simple speaker heads and mud pots. All these would be assembled and dismantled to try out different permutations and combinations of speakers and pots. He had a natural penchant for electronics.

The EEE department had fifty-four boys and six girls. Hari and his friends Mani, Malu and Nandhini joined EEE. Sara and her first-year friend, Jaisri made friends with this four-member group. Soon, the six-member group shared a strong bond. They studied, ate and walked around the college together. They used to share their knowledge and lunch. They used to divide the lessons into six portions, each one mastered one portion and taught their portion to the other five.

Sarayu and Hariharan would take the same bus and get down at the same bus stop. Hari's uncle's house was about a kilometer away from Sara's house. They had to walk together for 500 meters before parting at a junction.

Hari used to bring two lunch boxes – one for him and one for his friends. Most of the days, Sara's lunch would be from Hari's box. Her idli would be shared among others.

During study holidays, all the six would meet at Hari's place in the name of group studying. First, they would help him cook. After that, they would eat. Then they would rest and chat for a bit before finally settling down to study.

Sometimes, Hari's mother would come to stay with him for the weekend. She used to serve them delicious food. They used to find out that Hari's mom was in town, just by the aroma of cooking four or five houses away. So heavenly was the smell and taste of the food, and the love with which she served the children that they wished she would stay there forever.

In between eating, chatting and laughing, they prepared for the exams well. All of them scored fairly well in the third and fourth semesters, that is, in the second year of college.

Growing Up

Sarayu grew up between two boys; Srini was one-year older than her and Raghav was one-year younger. Their youngest sister, Yamuna was five-years younger to her.

During high school, Srini, Sara and Raghav used to play cricket with other boys their age in the street. Sometimes they would be chased from the street because of a broken window by some unforgiving neighbor. At such times, they used to go to the huge school playground, four streets away from home, to play cricket on weekends.

They would collect sticks from trees and use them as their stumps. If they could not find big enough sticks, four or five twigs tied together with twine would act as their stumps. They had to dig holes four inches deep to erect the stumps, and then reinforce them with a heap of mud tightly packed around them. When they began playing on Saturdays, they would do this and leave the stumps there to resume playing on Sundays.

Many teams used to play cricket in the huge field. Every team had an unofficial territory of their own. Usually, all the teams respected other teams' territory and kept to their respective areas. But sometimes, when they returned on Sundays, they found their stumps damaged, apparently by a lazy team who could not waste time or who did not know how to make stumps, and had used their pitch to play.

After vigorous brainstorming, Srini came up with a brilliant idea to safeguard their stumps. Sara and Raghav were also thrilled by the idea.

On a Saturday, before they left for the field, Srini took an old long record notebook and tore away its cardboard cover. He took some jute cord and a black color crayon.

After they finished playing, they waited until all the other teams left. Then, Srini took the crayon out and wrote on the cover in big letters.

> *'This belongs to a ghost.*
>
> *If you touch these stumps,*
>
> *I will come and possess you.*
>
> *– Yours sincerely,*
>
> GHOST'

Then he made two holes in the top corners of the cardboard using a sharp twig and put the ends of the cord through the holes and tied a knot. Then he carefully hung the board on the stump in the middle.

Then the three of them stood there, a few steps away from the stumps, admiring their work. The sun was setting in the west, but the three did not realize that it would become dark in a few minutes.

At that moment, they heard a familiar but odd voice screaming, "You, rascals," and a small pebble hit Sara's back. She was shocked and looked at Srini. He was also hit by another pebble and his face paled. They turned and saw the silhouette of a woman coming towards them half-walking and half-running. She was aiming, probably another pebble, at Raghav. Her hair was let loose.

The pebble hit Raghav. He winced.

Srini screamed "Ghost! Help!"

"No… it's mom!" Sara shouted.

Their mother was standing there, panting. She was very angry. Her face was red and her eyes were so furious that the three of them feared that they might burn to ashes.

"I have been searching for you for so long…you idiots! I went all over the place in search of you…and here you brats are playing cricket at this late hour in this isolated place! How dare you!" she was panting and shouting at the top of her lungs.

The three took to their heels. That evening, Sara received some extra thrashings as special reward for staying out after sunset and playing with the boys. Nevertheless, they rolled on the floor laughing whenever they recounted this story.

Hari visited his parents every weekend during his first year at college. In the second year, the number of visits dropped to one or two per month. On the weekends when he did not go to his native place, Hari used to join Sara, Srini and Raghav to play cricket. They would play either in the street or in the school playground. They would assemble after lunch and play until six O' clock in the evening. Hari and Srini became good friends. Both of them would talk for hours together about their future plans. They shared the same dream vehicle, a Hero Honda bike, which was of course the dream vehicle for most boys their age. Invariably, all the boys planned to buy a Hero Honda with their first salary.

Sara's father would invite Hari to lunch with them before playing. Sometimes, on hot summer days, they would play a game of *carrom* at home. Hari became a family friend. Even Sara's mother was friendly with him and was happy to have him over for lunch.

Sometimes, Srini, Hari and Sara used to take their bicycles and ride around the area near their college. Sara was fascinated by the hillock opposite to their college. The desire to climb the hillock grew exponentially in her. But Srini and Hari were not keen on the adventure. They advised her against the idea. But she resolved to climb to the top of the hillock one day.

One day, the six-member group sat in the college canteen sipping tea. The canteen overlooked the hillock. She told her friends how she wanted to climb it but Srini and Hari refused to oblige. The other four also advised her against the idea.

"I am going to climb it one day whether you five are coming with me or not," Sara announced to her friends.

Growing Up

"I will go with you, Sara," said a voice from behind them. The senior boys from the Mechanical department were standing there. It was Rahul; the boy who tried to rag Sara in vain on her first day of college. A few months prior, he had apologized to Sara about the incident and made friends with her.

"When Rahul? When can we go?" Sara was elated.

"Why not now?" Rahul asked dramatically spreading his hands and leaning towards her.

"Now?"

"Yes, now. I am ready if you are ready. Let's go."

Sara was thrilled. She gave her bag to her friends, who were looking at her disapprovingly.

"I will join you for lunch break. See you guys, bye."

Hari did not approve of her decision. "Bad idea," he said in a stern voice. But Sara had already started walking away with the boys.

Sara, Rahul and two of his friends went to the hillock. It took them about twenty minutes to reach the top. The rock was slippery in some places. Somehow they managed to reach the top.

They looked at their college from the top of the hillock and it was very picturesque! It was breath-taking! She could never forget it! They spent a good half-an-hour in the shade under the tree with bright yellow flowers, chatting about friends, joking and laughing. Then they climbed down and went back to the college.

The watchman greeted them at the small gate. "The Principal wants to meet you," he grinned.

They got an earful from the angry Principal. Sara did not understand why he had taken their harmless adventure so seriously.

"Who will answer to your parents if something happened to you? What if you slipped, fell down and broke a limb?" He turned to Sara, "You being a girl...how dare you go over there with boys! Bring your father to meet me tomorrow. I want to talk to him about your bad behavior."

Sara went home and narrated the whole story to her parents. Her mom was very furious about the episode. She started telling-off her father for Sara's brazenness. But her dad laughed when he heard the story.

"I will meet your Principal tomorrow morning, don't worry. But I think it is time you tamed your ways," he said.

'Tame my ways? What is wrong with dad? He has never been like this. If he were there, he would have climbed the hillock with me but he is asking to tame my ways!'

The next day, her dad went to college with her. The Principal knew that Sara's father was a high official in a state-government office and he received him with respect. Sara was asked to wait outside the Principal's room.

Inside the room, the Principal started to talk after the formal exchange of pleasantries.

"Sir, I am sure that you know what your daughter did yesterday. She would have reported it to you, I believe."

"Yes sir, she told me that she climbed the small hillock opposite the college."

"With some boys," the Principal said.

"Yes. She told me that too. Some senior boys from the Mechanical department, I believe."

The Principal was surprised by the fact that Sara's father had taken the incident so lightly.

"Don't you think that this is a dangerous thing to do, sir?"

"Sir, I am sorry for what she did. But, it is her nature; she is a tomboy. She is used to these adventures. I used to take her with my two sons on some adventurous picnics. I have brought her up like a boy. I do not discriminate between my sons and daughters."

The Principal did not expect this. He was amused.

"But sir, don't you see the downside of it? What if she slipped and broke a leg? What if the boys tried to misbehave with her using the privacy the hill top offers? Has she ever thought of these dangers?"

Sara's father was thoughtful for a couple of minutes.

"I would like to advise you to not let her do such things," the Principal said. "I hope you understand the seriousness of my concern."

Sara's father spoke apologetically. "Yes sir. I do understand that. And I appreciate your concern about your students very much. I will tell her not to resort to such dangerous adventures hereafter." He continued thoughtfully, "Sir, unlike other children, she has a tough life at home. My wife is particularly harsh to her. Sarayu is made to do all the household chores. She is not even fed properly by her mom."

The Principal could not believe his ears.

Sara's father continued, "I have tried my best to stop my wife from behaving like this…but it's in vain. If I chide her, she would wage an ugly war at home and make my life miserable."

"Err... I never heard of such a mother, sir..."

"Sara has survived this miserable childhood only because of her hyperactive, tomboyish attitude. So I do not control her intrepidity because it is saving her from becoming a dull, good-for-nothing mouse. Otherwise, she wouldn't be able to survive."

"You need not worry about her future, sir. She is a brilliant student. She will definitely do well in life and make you proud," the Principal had started to console the anxious father.

But Sara's father was now unstoppable. "My wife does not even allow her to study at home peacefully. But Sara made me proud by becoming the top scorer at her high school and at such a big school too. Did you know that about a 1000 students wrote the school finals with her?"

"Oh yes, sir. I know that the Vellore Government Girls' school is the biggest in the district." The Principal went on consoling Sara's father and assured him that Sara would indeed have a bright future.

Outside the room, Sara was wondering what was going on for such a long time. Was the Principal issuing a suspension order? Or worse, was she being dismissed from the college? So many worst case scenarios presented themselves in her mind as the minutes ticked by.

At last, the Principal and her dad came out of the room. They shook hands. "Bye sir. Take care," the Principal was smiling at her dad. He even sent a smile in Sara's direction. "Come and see me before going to class," he told her and went into his room.

'Oh! Well then. Nothing as bad as I feared has taken place. For dad's sake, I should not indulge in such immature activities hereafter.' She was relieved.

"What happened pa?" she asked as they walked out through the corridor. "What did the Principal say? What did you tell him?"

"Nothing. He expressed his concern about your safety. I told him that you are a brave girl and we used to go on adventures like this as a family. But Sara, there is a point to his fears. What if you slipped and broke something? For god's sake, don't do things like this hereafter."

"I won't, pa. I am sorry." He patted her back and left.

Sara went back to the Principal's office.

He started with a sarcastic smile, "So, Miss Tomboy, you are used to adventures like climbing hillocks, is it?"

"Sorry sir," Sara's face became pale. "I will not do this again."

"You better not. You be a brave girl or whatever. But do not resort to these activities as long as you are a student at this college. You may go to your class now."

"Thank you, sir!" Sara started to walk away with her head hanging.

"One more thing," his voice stopped her. "Do not spoil the poor boys, leave them alone." This remark embarrassed her thoroughly, "Yes, sir." with that she left the room.

Her friends were waiting for her in the corridor since it was the lunch break. She got an earful from them too.

"Serves you right," Hari said looking content. He was happier that he was proved right rather than feeling sorry for she had been admonished by the Principal.

Chapter 2

TUMBLING DOWN

The third-year of the diploma course consisted of two semesters; the fifth and sixth. They were called the final semesters. For getting a first-class diploma, one has to score an average above sixty percent on the first attempt. If your score is below sixty and above fifty percent, you will be awarded a second-class diploma. Failing a paper or being absent for an exam but managing to get more than a sixty percent average still results in a second-class diploma. A first-class diploma ensured a placement in the state-government-owned Electricity Board for electrical and electronics students. Even if they missed out on employment there, there were other premium public sector employers. For second-class diploma engineers, life would become very difficult. They would be thrown to less-privileged employment sectors with private companies that preferred to pay less. It was said that people in these places worked harder and for longer hours too.

So, naturally, all the final-year students got very serious about their studies. They put in extra hours for group study and discussions, while the first and second-year students enjoyed cultural and sports activities.

It was fifth semester for our six-member gang. Their extra-curricular activities were reduced, playfulness subdued and study time increased. Everything went very well for Sara until a month before the final exams of fifth semester. Then all hell broke lose. At first, it started as mild fever stints. The frequency and severity of the fever increased as days passed. Her friends urged her to see a doctor.

But her mother decided that she could do with paracetamols. Why waste money on a doctor for a simple fever? She was deaf to the incessant coughing through the night. She never bothered to check if Sara ate or not so she did not notice that her intake was decreasing and at times she skipped her meals.

The very thought of food made Sara puke. On some days, a glass of milk with a slice of bread was all she ate the whole day. Everyone in college noticed that she was terribly sick and enquired if she had done any tests and what the results said.

From a very tender age, Sara had suspected that her mom was very different from other moms. Unlike other moms, her mom was always very harsh to her. But she was so sweet to Raghav and Yamuna; they were the prince and princess of the household. Her elder brother, Srini, fell somewhere between these two categories. She was sometimes-harsh and sometimes-kind to her elder son. But she was always mean to Sara. She used Sara like a dartboard to vent her anger and she seemed to be angry twenty-four/seven.

Sara had slowly been trained to do all the household chores. At the age of eight, she started sweeping and mopping the house. At nine, she was washing dishes and washing her clothes. At ten, she was made to wash her sister's clothes too.

The family used to have idli for breakfast everyday. So, every evening, after coming home from school, Sara had to grind the batter for idli with the stone mortar and pestle.

She was also the coffee grinder operator for her mom. Mom used to have freshly-brewed coffee four times a day. She loved exotic coffee so much that she used to buy superior coffee beans from a particular vendor. She roasted the beans once in two days in a specially designated pan.

The coffee grinder was made of wrought iron. This was a machine one could find in any coffee-lover's home. It was a one-foot tall machine. Two inches above the bottom of the machine, it had a jaw-like opening and at the bottom of it, there was a screw to secure it to any surface it was fixed to. They had a wooden stool on which this machine was fixed for grinding sessions. The roasted beans would be fed a fistful at a time into a square mouth at the top of the machine. There would be a handle on the side which had to be turned manually so that the gear system would rotate, take in the beans and crush them in the crusher attached to the handle. This coffee grinding was Sara's responsibly on most days. Sometimes, when she had lots of vessels to clean or clothes to wash, one of her brothers would be deputed to do the job.

The family did not have enough income to employ a maid to do the housework… In those days, daughters helping mothers with these chores was a common thing. But it usually started when they were about fourteen-years-old.

But Sara's case was a rare one; neighborhood ladies used to discuss it in hushed voice. They were afraid of earning her mother's wrath. Sara realized that this behavior at home was unusual only from their gossiping.

Occasionally, if a kind-hearted lady in the neighborhood attempted to make mom realize that Sara was too young to do these tasks, she would promptly be shunned by mom. She used to snap at this intruder, "I know what is good and what is bad for my child. If you have any other work to do, it's better you go and attend to it."

Any new neighbor would be duly warned by other ladies, so that they don't attempt to educate mom on how to handle her kids.

Sara had received a hug from her mother only once in her life. Most days, she was like a punching bag for her. Mom's favorite method of inflicting pain was to strike Sara's head with a clenched fist; it would feel like she had bee hit by a thunderbolt. Sometimes, it would pain for two to three days. It was a miracle that her brain was not damaged by all those punches.

It was made crystal clear to her at a very young age that her chores had to be finished before she left for school or college, whether it was a normal day or the day of an exam. If and only if she finished her chores, she could step outside. Similarly, as soon as she returned from school, she had to grind idli batter, wash the vessels, and cut vegetables before she could go out to play or study. She had to mop the floor twice a week. The family used to have dinner together; arranging the plates and cleaning them after dinner were all Sara's job.

In school and college, Sara did her best to hide the facts of her gloomy scenario at home. She would pretend like nothing was ever wrong with her life. Sometimes, when her teachers or classmates noticed a small bump on her forehead inflicted by that clenched fist, she would invent a story about how she got injured while playing or slipped while walking. The more she was ill-treated at home, the more authoritative and tomboyish she grew in the outside world. The fact that she could score well by just listening in class, without putting in extra effort at home made her more confident with each passing day, to the point she was called a proud girl.

Her mom would never let her sit and study at home peacefully. She would rather have her do some chore. She used to tell her, "You need not become a collector and provide my livelihood when I am old. It's enough if you are a useful daughter now and finish your chores." In spite of that, Sara ended up being the school topper. Not just in school but she also scored the highest marks in the history of both her mother's and father's families.

The Headmistress of her school advised her to continue in the same school for the eleventh and twelfth grade and join an engineering college after that. But Sara had her own reason for joining this diploma course. She had to find a shortcut, had to earn and stand on her own two legs at the earliest. She had to do whatever it took to escape from her vicious mother at the earliest. She had to flee her miserable home the first chance she got, even if it meant leaving her loving dad.

For her, two years higher-secondary followed by a four-year long degree was too much time to endure the harsh life at home. She consoled herself that there was always the possibility of getting into a part-time degree program after the diploma. The prospect of having a prestigious degree did not seem important to her at that point of time. All she wanted was freedom.

The one and only time Sara got a hug and a kiss from mom was the day the tenth grade results came. Yes! Mom hugged her and planted a kiss on her cheek in a sudden surge of pride. But it was just momentary. The next day, when dad said she could join the diploma course, mom fought tooth and nail against it.

"If you let her become an engineer, then you will have to search for an engineer groom for her and spend a lot on her wedding. This will bring us plenty of suffering," she warned dad.

"If I give her good education, she will earn enough money for her wedding." For once, dad was firm with his decision. He was not going to allow his ruthless wife to spoil the future of his daughter. After all, it was a government institute and they did not have to spend too much on her education unlike what his better-half said.

Once Sara asked her father if she was really born to mom or they had picked her up from a road side garbage bin or an orphanage. He laughed at the question and assured her that she was indeed born to her mother. He went on to describe how her mother went into prolonged labor to deliver a tiny, under-weight pre-mature baby at seven months, how the chance of Sara's survival was put at fifty-fifty by the doctor, and how she became a chubby baby in six months with mom's care.

One evening, ten days before the fifth semester final exams, Sara returned home from college and vomited blood. Her mother was so horrified by the sight of blood that she immediately took her to the government hospital.

The doctor there got admitted her to the emergency ward immediately. He suspected it was an advanced stage of Tuberculosis and told her mother that they would do some tests the next day and she needed to be at the hospital at least for a week. He asked her to go home and bring clothes and other necessities to stay with her. Her mother said ok and went home but never returned to see her for her entire ten-day stint at the hospital. Instead, her father came in the evening to sign the forms for the treatments to begin.

Her father used to come every morning on the way to the office with a glass of Bournvita from home. He would stay with her for half-an-hour. Then he would come again in the evenings on his way back home and spend around two hours with her. Since it was a women's ward, he could not stay with her during the night. Her mother did not want to stay with her because the government hospital was the poorest and dirtiest medical facility in town. She could not bring herself to set foot in such a filthy place even for Sara's sake.

Sara was left in the care of the hospital staff. But they were all generally very kind to her and took good care of her. They used to ask her father why her mother or any other female relative did not stay with her. He had to make up lame excuses like one of the other children was not feeling well, and his wife had to stay at home to take care of that child. But sooner or later, the people around them understood her mother's nature and took pity on her.

All her friends from college visited her at the hospital, some of the girls started weeping when they saw Sara in a zombie-like state. Her lecturers also came to see her at the hospital. Hari used to come to the hospital everyday after college, sit with her for an hour or so and teach her for the exam. But her mother never came to see her. All that she did was send the Bournvita and an occasional box of dal and rice with her father.

She was diagnosed with a severe case of TB. It was so severe that she could have died if they had delayed treatment for a few more days. She was advised to take a set of tablets for the next six months. This treatment was a pilot project facilitated by government hospitals across the country to eradicate TB.

Two days before her discharge from the hospital, Krishnan came to visit her at the hospital. Krishnan was a heartthrob at college. He was in the same year as Sara but in the Mechanical Engineering department. He shared the number one rank in academics with his close friend, Ravi. Krishnan and Ravi took part in singing and dancing events at cultural college events. Sara shared the stage with them during those events. Both Krishnan and Ravi were good friends with Sara.

Krishan gave her an elaborate bouquet of roses. The card on the bouquet was handwritten and it read,

> *'Get well soon, dear Sara.*
>
> *With Love*
>
> *Krishnan'*

The word 'love' was underlined with a florescent pen in a wavy pattern.

She was surprised and looked at him. He gave her a meaningful look. He took her hand in his, held it tightly and said, "Please get well soon. I will be waiting for you." He blushed as he said those words and left the room at once, without even turning to look at her one more time.

Sara felt butterflies fluttering in her stomach for a while. She loved the feeling and wanted to have more of it.

She was discharged just two days before her exams. She decided to sit for the exams. Even if she was absent for the exams, it meant a second-class diploma. Why not try writing something instead? But she could not sit for the entire three hours for any of the exams. She could not think clearly and felt dizzy most of the time due to her medication.

When the exam results came, she failed two papers. It meant that she had to clear the arrears along with the sixth semester papers or in the following semester.

This was her first failure in life. It was quite devastating. Now, her secret dream of enrolling at an engineering college for a part-time degree was shattered. One needed a first-class diploma to get admission for a degree course at any of the reputed government colleges. Her chances of getting a good job were also very bleak now.

She was not new to handling hardship. She had been a fighter right from birth. She was a pre-mature baby, born at seven months and was given a fifty-fifty chance of survival by the doctors. From that day onward, her life was a long battle to overcome all sorts of odds.

But the TB attack was an entirely different battle.

She was advised to come to the hospital for two days a week for the next six months to take her medicine. There, they would give her a packet consisting of eleven tablets of different sizes, shapes and colors. She had to swallow them in front of the head nurse. They would give only that day's medicine. They would not let the patients take the medicine home.

The days she took tablets were hell. Her body would become shaky. She wouldn't be able to eat properly and feel nauseous throughout the day. She suffered throughout her sixth semester in this state.

But at the end of six months, when the tests were done, she was completely cured of TB. She was the first patient in the history of the hospital's TB cell to be cured completely in six months. She had religiously taken the tablets, come what may, unlike the other patients. The doctor was very happy for her.

From week one, Hari used to accompany her for the hospital visits. He used to take out the tablets one by one and put them in her palm to swallow. He would make sure that she took all eleven tablets. Then he would accompany her to the bus stop, carried her bag, helped her get on the bus and saw that she was seated comfortably. After college, he would walk the extra distance to her house, leave her at home safely and then go to his house.

Without Hari, Sara would never have made it. He used to bring her nutritious and delicious food for lunch. He accompanied her to the numerous blood tests, MMR sessions and doctor reviews.

It was the sixth and final semester for them. Sara decided to concentrate only on her sixth semester papers. She could not take the extra load of the two arrear papers. She would take those exams later with the next batch of students. It was going to be a second-class diploma only anyhow. Why be bothered then? The door to a bright future had already been closed to her. What was the point in working hard anymore?

Her friends kept cheering her up and assuring her that all was not lost just because she missed out on a first-class diploma. Their group studies continued as usual. Hari took up Sara's portions to study and teach the rest of the gang.

The day of the final exams arrived. It was a Monday. They had three exams per week and so it would all be over in three weeks.

Hari's mother had stayed with him for the past one week to help him cope with the exam preparations. Hari and his friends were feasting on her meals, snacks and tea. Even when she prepared simple buttermilk for them, it tasted heavenly.

She had to leave on the day of his first exam. She had to go back and get his brothers and sister ready for their school and college. They had their final exams that day too. April is the month of exams for almost all the educational institutions across the country. Mother was torn between him and his siblings. She was preparing to leave half-heartedly.

She had woken up very early in the morning, prepared dal and curry for him. She had to catch the six O' clock bus to reach home before seven-thirty. She had to cook breakfast for her children before they left for school.

"Hari, be sure to read the questions properly before answering. Be careful and write the exams well."

"Ma, don't worry. I have prepared extremely well for the exams. I went through the question banks of the past three years and prepared answers to all the probable questions. It's me who taught my friends the answers to many important questions."

His mother was proud of Hari. She always had been. He was the most brilliant among all her children. He made the family proud by topping his school in the tenth grade. However small the school was, a 'school topper' is a 'school topper'.

"Hari, it is getting late. Go and fetch an auto to take me to the bus stand. I have put the water on the stove. It will take ten minutes to boil. Put the rice in after it starts boiling and let it cook."

"Ma, I know. I've been cooking here all these years, I mean, when you are not here."

Hari took his bicycle and went out in search of an auto. He could not find one nearby. Finally, he found one a few streets away and brought it home. She was waiting at the door. She ruffled his hair before getting into the auto.

"Take care, Hari. Write the exams well. Amma will be waiting for you to come home once the exams are over." and she left. Hari was waving his hand until the auto disappeared at the end of the street.

Hari went inside the house and into the kitchen to check the water for the rice. It was already boiling. He put the washed rice into the vessel. The dal and curry had already been prepared and packed by his mother. He waited until the rice was cooked, switched off the stove, placed the lid with holes on top of the vessel, grabbed the mouth of the vessel and took it to the sink. He drained the excess water through the holes in the lid by tilting the vessel at an angle. After that he had to place a block of wood underneath the lid and let it stand, so that the rest of the water completely drained.

Supporting the vessel with one hand, he groped for the wooden block and suddenly it slipped and toppled over his right palm, pouring the entire thing on the back of his palm.

He was paralysed by the shock and pain. He winced and extracted his hand from under the vessel. The pain was excruciating. He placed his palm under running water but the pain did not subside. The skin on the back of his palm turned an alarming beetroot color. The skin came off in some places and the white flesh showed.

He ran outside screaming and knocked on his neighbor's door. The gentleman was shocked when he saw his palm. He quickly brought out a towel soaked in cool water and wrapped it around the palm. He took Hari to a nearby doctor on his bike.

The doctor gave him a painkiller, cleaned his wound, applied a cream generously and bandaged the palm. He prescribed some medicine for three days and asked Hari to see him after a week. The kind neighbor rode him back home. When he came back home, he realized that it was eight-thirty. His friends would have gathered at their usual place in the garden. They would be wondering and worrying why he did not turn up for the exam.

Good grief! He wouldn't be able to write the exam with a bandaged right hand. Going by the severity of the wound, he might not write any of the exams in the next three weeks. The thought of losing a first-class diploma made him dizzy.

He slumped in a chair. Tears rolled down his cheeks. He wanted to see his mother immediately. He started to pack some clothes into a bag with his left hand. He wanted to go home.

But his friends would be worried about him. He had to tell them before leaving. He ate his breakfast, took his medicine, put the leftover food in the refrigerator, took his suitcase, locked the house with his left hand, got an auto and went to the bus stop.

He went to the college and waited in the garden outside the exam hall where he and his friends used to assemble after every exam. He was sitting on the bench in the shade of a big tree, thinking about his future.

'The probability of getting employed in the Electricity Board is zero now. My parents are dreaming of a financially stable and safe life for me! I was dreaming of enrolling in a part-time degree course after getting a good job! All the dreams were shattered in a matter of minutes! What will my father say? How will my mother react? They will be shattered over this misfortune.'

The students started to come out of the exam halls. All his friends were walking towards him with a confused look. They were shocked when they saw his hand. Hari was overwhelmed by emotion and started to cry when he saw them.

He told them what happened in the morning. All of them were very upset. The happiness of doing the paper very well had vanished for all of them. The girls started to cry too.

Why? Of all people in the world, why is god being this cruel to Hari? And to Sara last semester?' they wondered and discussed this. But to Sara, the question did not make any sense, because she was an atheist. For her, the words 'god' and 'fate' were all rubbish. There was no such thing as god and he certainly was not responsible for the happenings.

They consoled each other. Hari had lunch with his friends and left for his hometown. He was not going to write the rest of the exams too. What was the point of staying in Vellore? Mother would take care of him if he went home.

"Don't worry guys. I will be back for the last day of the college," he assured them and left.

Sara was the most upset of them all. She knew exactly how Hari was feeling at the moment. She knew what it was to be affected by bad luck.

The rest of them did all their other papers well. They missed Hari very much.

After finishing the last exam, Sara came out of the hall and walked towards the garden for her usual rendezvous with her team. She saw Ravi from the Mechanical department approaching her.

"Hi Sara, how did you write the exams?"

"Very well, Ravi. I am sure to get above eighty-five percent in all the papers."

"Wow. Good to hear that."

"What good is that going to be? I will get a second-class diploma only irrespective of the good marks I score now or in the fifth semester arrear clearance after six months."

"Hey Sara, don't lose heart. You will have a bright future for sure. The lucky guy that marries you will treat you like a queen. You will not suffer just because you got a second-class diploma."

Sara burst into laughter. "Like a queen! First let's see who will be ready to marry me? Then we can think about being treated like a queen!"

"Why, Sara! I would like to be that lucky guy. I mean, if you could consider it," Ravi said.

"What the…"

"Believe me, Sara, I gave you my heart the moment I saw you on the first day of college. I wanted to secure my future before I let you know about it. After all, I needed to be in a position to give you a good life, before asking for your consent to marry me."

"But, Ravi…" Sara stopped. How could she tell Ravi that his best friend, Krishnan expressed his love for her when she was in the hospital and since that day she had butterflies in her stomach whenever she saw Krishnan? She liked the feeling, and longed to have more of it.

Krishnan and she had been exchanging secret glances though both of them did not talk about what had happened. Sara could not define what it was that she felt about Krishnan.

'Does Ravi know about Krishnan? They are very close friends. Is it possible that they did not talk about me? Something does not tally.'

"You know, Ravi… Krishnan was…"

"Yes. He told me about you and his 'get well' card. I know that he is smitten with you. But, it would be unfair if I don't get a chance to express my love for you. I was the one who met you first on the first day of college. I fell in love with you the moment I saw you that day."

Sara did not know whether to laugh or take pity on him. She never thought that Ravi would have fostered such foolish thoughts. He was a practical guy. He had set definite goals in his life about his higher studies, about earning well and settling big, and giving a happy retired life to his widowed mother. She always liked him; respected him for his brilliance and studiousness but only as a good friend.

'What's with the boys these days? Losing hearts to girls at the drop of a hat! Why do such thoughts come to them? I never seem to be interested in boys!'

"Sorry Ravi. I do not have the luxury of thinking about love and marriage, at least until I turn twenty-five. I don't want to think about that till I achieve something worthy in my life, career and higher studies. Forgive me. I am sorry. I have to decline your proposal. Do not waste your time. Get a good job, earn well, marry a good match and get settled in life."

"I can wait for you, Sara…"

"No. You will NOT. Please. Leave me alone. This is not the time for me to think or talk about marriage. We are too young for that. We have lots to do in life before thinking of marriage. Please understand. Good bye."

Ravi was expecting this from her. He was not at all disappointed.

"It's ok. I will ask for your hand in marriage when you turn twenty-five. For now, I am happy that I have revealed my feelings to you. Whenever you feel like thinking about marriage, please think of me first." he said matter-of-factly.

"Oh! Good! Let us see then. Let me see if you remember my twenty-fifth birthday first," Sara laughed. Ravi joined in her laughter.

Six months later, Sara and Hari sat for their arrear clearance exams along with many habitual arrear writers. Ram, a timid boy from their class was among them. Ram was waiting with Hari to see Sara when she finished her last exam and came out of the hall.

"Sara, Ram wants to say goodbye to you since this is your last exam and he won't be able to see you hereafter, he wanted to meet you," said Hari.

"Oh! That's nice of you, Ram. Good luck with your diploma, I hope you get it at the earliest." Sara turned to Hari and asked, "Shall we go Hari?"

"Ram wants to talk to you. You both keep talking. I will go to the canteen and buy us snacks." Hari left for the canteen.

'What is there for Ram to talk to me alone? Something fishy is going on.'

From the familiar look on Ram's face, which she had seen in many boys over the past three years, she could guess what could be the 'talk' was about.

'Wait. Do not jump to conclusions. He may want to talk about anything. It need not be what you think,' she thought.

Ram came from a faraway small village. He was an introvert. He always kept to himself in his hostel room. He made friends with only a couple of boys; Hari was one of them. Ram had arrears in almost all the semesters; there were at least three papers per semester. It looked like he would take at least a year or two to clear all his papers. The irony was that the boy was a school topper in high school with a centum in mathematics. His father was the headmaster of the school at which he studied. He came from an affluent family.

The family was hoping to produce the first engineer from their clan.

Ram produced an autograph book and asked for her signature. This was a regular practice among the students; getting everyone's signature in their autograph books.

Then, he fished out an eighty-page notebook from his bag with trembling hands. He hesitantly gave the notebook to her.

"What is this Ram?"

"It's a collection of poems I wrote over the past three years."

"Wow. You write poems? I never knew that!" she took the notebook from him.

"Please read it, Sara."

"Of course I will. I love Tamil. I like to read. I like poems. I will read it leisurely," she proceeded to put the notebook in her bag.

"Sara...would you mind reading them now and returning the notebook to me?"

"Why? I have to leave now. Hari is waiting for me. We have to go home for lunch."

"Please... Sara. Hari will come back only after twenty minutes. He said that he will buy us some snacks and tea." His eyes were pleading. "I cannot part with the notebook. I mean, I have written everything in this notebook only. I have no other copies..."

"Oh! Is that so? In that case, I will read it now," Sara sat on a bench and started reading his poems. Ram sat on a bench opposite to her, bent over and looked at his fingernails.

The poems were written in Tamil. Though it was a collection of assorted poems, a story was told through them. It spoke about Ram in the first person, and a girl, Sita. He sees the girl, falls in love with her, gets married, has children, and so on and so forth. Some of the poems described and admired Sita's eyes, lips, hair and even her nails. In some poems he was worshiping her singing, dancing, cooking, etc. He described what a loveable and loving wife she was. There were some intimate scenes as well between Ram and Sita. He even named his children and sent them to school. Oh! Finally the story ended with both Ram and Sita becoming very old, in their death beds, holding each other's hands, as death embraced them.

Sara was surprised that Ram possessed such a great hidden talent. She appreciated the poems with an occasional 'Good!', 'Wow!', etc while reading them.

"How is it possible to imagine an entire life with an imaginary person Ram? Wow. You can become a famous writer, you know? Is this Sita an imaginary person? It looks like there really is someone in your life. Your descriptions are so vivid." she admired the work.

"Thank you, Sara. I am glad that you liked it." Then he sat near her and took the notebook from her. He opened the back cover of the notebook and carefully removed a clip that held the last page and the back cover together. "Now, read this last page too." He thrust the notebook into her hand and went back to his place on the bench opposite.

The last page was written in red ink. The writing was thick and rough like it was written with a watercolor brush.

It read,
> 'These are not poems my dear;
>
> But drops of my blood.
>
> My lover is not an imaginary person, sweetheart;
>
> It is YOU'

'Oh my goodness! It is not red ink! It is blood! What the hell!' the notebook slipped from her hands. Ram lunged forward to save the falling notebook before it touched the ground. She froze and was speechless for a few minutes. Ram! Of all people in the world, Ram! Why? How? Ram was just an acquaintance, nothing more than that. They had not even spoken to each other for an hour in the three years.

'What is it with these boys! Why do they behave like this! Is it just their age?' She was overwhelmed with pity. By this point, rejecting love proposals had become such a routine ritual to Sara that she had become quite proficient in the art.

"Sorry Ram. I had no idea that you had these feelings for me. I was just being a good friend to you and I thought of you as a good friend only, nothing more than that."

"Sara, it's okay if you have not thought of me like that so far. But I beg you to consider accepting my love for you. If you say yes, I promise, you will be the happiest wife in the world. I will live up to your expectations."

"I am so sorry, Ram. It's better you stop this ridiculousness and start being practical. First, clear all your arrears and get your diploma, get a job and take care of yourself. Then you may start thinking of taking care of another human being." She wondered if she was being too harsh on him and stopped.

Hari returned with a tray with tea and snacks. Sara returned the notebook to Ram and started talking to him like nothing unusual had happened.

By the time Hari and Sara got their diplomas with eighty and eighty-five percent respectively, all four of their friends were employed by the Electricity Board.

For Hari and Sara, there was simply no point in getting registered in the employment exchange. None of the government organizations or the public sector units would consider them for a job. But they did register as a mere formality. Now, they had to start applying for the small and private establishments. They would consider second-class diplomas since they preferred to pay less than a standard salary. It would take decades for the two of them to climb up the ladder in any organization.

Why? Why them? What sin did they commit to deserve such a horrible punishment? Were they destined to fail? Were they not supposed to have a decent living? Just three years ago, both of them came to college as proud school toppers, with lots of dreams of a bright future, of a degree, of well-paid jobs. All those were thrown away today. All other average and just-above-average students got good employments. Did god let them down? Sara was not sure about the god factor, because, she was an atheist.

They started applying to small private companies in Chennai. They decided to seek jobs in the capital city. They would find more opportunities in Chennai than any other place in the state.

Chapter 3

SETTING FOOT

July, 1998

After four months of applying to more than two dozen jobs, Hari got an offer as a Trainee Hardware Engineer with a Personal Computer dealer in Chennai. He was lucky to get a job which he liked very much though the pay was not enough to meet even his basic needs. He had to continue getting financial support from his parents.

He could not afford a room in Chennai so he had to travel to Vellore by train after work everyday, take his bicycle which was parked at the railway station and cycle to his uncle's house in Vellore for eight kilometers. It would be eleven O' clock when he finished his supper and went to bed. The next morning, he would wake up at four, cook, pack his breakfast and lunch, cycle to the railway station, catch the train to Chennai and reach his office by 9 O' clock. His brothers stayed with him in Vellore to pursue their higher studies there. They helped him cook and pack his lunch.

Sara had to wait for another two months before being called for an interview. The vacancy was for a 'Trainee Technical Assistant', she had no clue what it meant. 'Beggars cannot be choosers, so you better not ask for details and rub the probable employer the wrong way,' she decided. The interview over the telephone went on well; a salary of 350 to start with was fixed. Her to-be boss promised if he was happy with her performance, he would increase the salary. He asked her to join the following Monday.

It was arranged with her uncle in Chennai that she would stay in his house as a paying guest for a month before she moved into a ladies' hostel. She went to Chennai on Sunday. She was too exhausted after the four-hour journey from Vellore to Chennai Central by bus and from there to her uncle's place. She reached their house in the evening. She could not sleep well on the couch in a new house. The excitement and anxiety kept her awake throughout the night.

She woke up at 5 O' clock on Monday, had a quick bath and breakfast, took the bus and reached Triplicane an hour before her reporting time. It was near Marina beach. Hari had told her over the phone that he would meet her at the bus stop and help her find the office. Sara could not go to a new place alone. She was topographically-challenged. Hari knew this very well and would not let her go in search of her workplace on her own.

Hari was waiting for her at the bus stop. His 'small town boy' look had changed a lot. The 'dripping with oil' hairstyle had changed to a stylish shampooed hairdo. He had developed the habit of pushing the hair to the side in such a way that it fell right back on his forehead. His loose village-style shirt had changed into a well-fitting, full sleeved one that was tucked in neatly, which complemented his six-foot frame. He used many English words while conversing. City boy!

Hari's office was a couple of stops away from her bus stop. They searched and found her office in a dirty narrow street, which was inappropriately named Big Street. It was on the first floor of one among many dirty commercial buildings that lined Big Street. Hari left her at the entrance after checking that that was the right place and went to catch his bus.

Sara went upstairs to 'Micro Circuits' and reported to her boss. Mr. Raj was a middle-aged man about five-feet tall with a big paunch, intelligent eyes, a receding hairline and a good sense of humor. He was the owner, manager and chief engineer of the unit. He was an electronics engineer; he conceived and designed the circuits for the instruments Micro Circuits produced. Timer and process controls for tire manufacturing units were the two major products.

There was a twenty-by-twenty hall for production, a small cabin inside the hall for the boss, a ten-by-twenty room for keeping raw materials and finished goods. All the places were generally dirty. There were two more girls who had joined a couple of months ago and two boys who were seniors by a year to them. There was also a handyman who was over thirty-years old.

Raj liked Sara on her first day. In a few days, she picked up soldering and testing. The five-foot, puny little girl surprised him with her swift learning and hard work. She was a perfectionist with a systematic approach to everything she did. Just two weeks after she joined, he taught her a

Setting Foot

valuable skill. She did not know at that time that this very skillset was going to propel her career and be the key to a successful future. He taught PCB artwork designing to her.

PCB, or printed circuit board is the functional map of an electronic circuit. It is the hardware of, in other words, the realization of any electronic instrument or gadget. The circuit is converted into the physical space which holds the components and establishes connections between the components.

To design a PCB for any circuit, one should understand the circuit, the current and voltage ratings, the thickness of the tracks required for the connections, and so on. A PCB designer should be thorough with the physical dimensions and configurations of each and every component used in the circuit. One has to integrate all this information and apply aesthetic sense while designing a PCB. The space constraints of the product play a major role in the design.

Since engineering drawing was her strongest subject in college, Sara picked up the skill very fast to Raj's delight. He was very happy with her meticulous work and slowly started giving her more complicated circuits. She was happily designing new circuits every few days.

The other two girls, Chitra and Dhana, were given the monotonous job of soldering hundreds of the same boards every day. The two boys were sent out to do fieldwork. Their job was to install and troubleshoot the units on-site. All the six of them shared the quality-check work. And the handyman's job was to pack the units and deliver them to the sites. He also did the cleaning and other errands like buying tea for the staff twice a day from across the street.

They shared one restroom with four or five more offices in the same building which was always in a pathetic condition. This was one thing Sara hated about the office. She dreamed of a posh office with neat and clean cabins and corridors like the ones she saw in TV serials. But her colleagues seemed blissfully oblivious to the condition of the restroom. Either they got used to it or that was the regular standard to them.

The office hours for both Hari and Sara were nine-thirty to six. Hari would meet her at the bus stop at eight-thirty near her office; they would walk across to Marina beach, spend about half-hour and then go to their respective offices. They eagerly looked forward to their morning meetings at the beach every day.

In 1988, designing PCB artwork was done manually. The artwork designer has to design the basic circuit in a graph sheet, place component after component, pin-by-pin and then draw connections between components track-by-track. Three different colors for each layer are used. Red for the top layer, blue for the bottom layer and black for the multilayer (the objects appearing in both the top and bottom layers). This basic design on a graph sheet takes anywhere between a day and a few weeks depending upon the size and complexity of the circuit.

Then the designer fixes a transparent sheet, which is called an artwork sheet, over the graph sheet. There are adhesive tapes of various widths in red, blue and black color. These are for the tracks. And, there are pads, which are black color stickers in the shape of donuts, available in various diameters. The pads are for the pins or legs of the components.

The designer sticks the pads where the components' pins are located and then runs the tapes for tracks establishing connections between the components. Again, this process takes anywhere between one day and a few weeks. The design on the graph sheet and the artwork sheet are plotted in 2x size, that is, double the actual size.

This artwork sheet is sent for making films of 1x size, that is, the actual size of the PCB. The films are sent to the PCB fabricators to make tens or hundreds or thousands of PCBs. The PCB artwork is the most revered object of any electronics design unit.

As the days and weeks went by, Raj started relying on Sara's abilities as a designer that he stopped supervising her work. He shifted the entire load of designing to her and started to concentrate on R&D (research and development). She was given a raise of 100 rupees from the second month. But, two souls were very unhappy because of these developments in the office. Chitra and Dhana did not appreciate the fact that their junior was getting all these accolades and salary hikes.

Chitra and Dhana were staying in a nearby hostel. They used to stick to each other almost the time at the office. They used to chat in low voices while assembling PCBs, gossiping about their hostel mates and cinema stories. These matters never interested Sara and she used to mind her design business.

She had her own set of problems. The uncomfortable atmosphere at the hostel where she was staying – she could not afford a better hostel; having to catch crowded buses in the mornings; half-drained energy levels by the time she reached her stop; and not enough and definitely not good food in the hostel. Adding to her woes was her broken English. The people in the city were in love with English. Wherever she went, they used the foreign language more than their mother tongue; speaking in Tamil put you in a poor light. Her only solace amidst this hardship was that she got to meet Hari every morning at the beach. What a time to meet! Nine O' clock at the beach under the scorching sun! But undeterred by the heat, they continued meeting every morning. This kept them going strong.

Hari was also doing well and earning a very good name at his office, 'PC Link'. His superiors at the office admired his sharpness and smartness. He was a favorite among his clients too.

Everything seemed to be going smoothly. Sara did not realize that one of her distant relatives was spying on her until he met her at the bus stop one day. The self-appointed Sherlock Holmes informed her that he knew she was meeting a boy at the beach every morning. He threatened to report her to her parents and make them take her back to Vellore. Though Sara was not worried about the news reaching her parents, she was disturbed by the fact that a person had been watching her without her knowledge. She was annoyed by the language he used and the implied threat of jeopardizing her career. He also threatened that he would spread the news among her relatives in Chennai and this would spoil her name and future. No one would marry her, he warned. What was his problem with her meeting a boy? He described 'meeting the boy' in a mean way in Tamil.

She could not give her usual one hundred percent undivided attention to the design she was doing that week. It was a version upgrade of an old design. All hell broke lose when 50 PCBs of the design arrived a few days later.

Mr. Raj unpacked the parcel and inspected the PCBs. Suddenly, he shouted in disbelief, "Sarayu! What the hell is this?" Her heart skipped a beat and she rushed to his cabin. What was it that made him so angry?

"Look what you have done!" he threw one of the PCBs on the table and pointed at the main IC (integrated circuit, ICs are chips with specific functions).

She immediately saw her folly. She designed the IC as viewed from the component side instead of from solder side. She forgot to reverse the patterns for the solder side-view. He looked at the board and her alternately with disdain. She began to perspire profusely. Her mouth went dry. She stood there dumbstruck. She had never felt like this before in her life.

The time was lost, money was lost and they had to deliver the finished product in two days. Correcting the artwork would take her at least eight hours. And there also be time for fabrication. That would take a minimum of three days. Tears rolled down her cheeks. She was ashamed of herself. 'How could you make such a silly mistake! The PCBs are going to go to waste because of your carelessness!' she was overwhelmed with self-reproach.

However, two people were secretly happy about the episode; Chitra and Dhana. Sarayu was treated like a superior being; it was like she was the only one with brains. Serves her right! Now she has fallen from her height.'

Raj was very smart and strong when it came to his subject. He raked his brain for two hours, referred to some data books and found another IC whose configuration somewhat matched with the messed-up design. With a few cuts in the tracks and a few additions he made the prototype work. What a relief to Sara! And of course, to Raj! All the fifty boards underwent the cut-and-wire process and they managed to deliver the instruments with a delay of just two days.

Chitra and Dhana were always rude to Sara, well not always but most of the time. Sometimes, Chitra used to talk to her nicely. She used to tell Sara and Dhana about the interviews she attended with bigger companies over the weekends.

One day she told Sara that she was offered a salary of 750 per month in Kody's. She used to conclude her interview episodes with a declaration that she was going to resign the following month after receiving the month's salary. But the resignation never really happened. By the time she received that month's salary, there would be another story about another company offering her a better salary doing its rounds.

A regular conversation would go like, "Sara, I am going to resign next Saturday. But I am afraid of telling, Raj sir."

"Why? What are you afraid of?"

"How can I go and tell him that I am leaving this company for another for a higher salary?"

"Why? What's wrong with that? If you think what you are doing is right, what stops you from telling him?"

"No. How can I tell him? I am afraid of him. I will simply stop coming to work after taking this month's salary."

"That is up to you. But, if I were you, I would notify to him in a polite way and resign in a proper way. I would not disappear just like that after taking salary."

'Stupid girl. Why am I telling her all this? So that she might go tell him. And he will consider a hike to retain me. Instead, she is preaching to me about what to tell and how to resign. This dumb girl is a waste of time. There is absolutely no use talking to her,' Chitra would revoke the idea of talking to Sara for at least a week.

Hari got a promotion and a hike in PC Link. He started to earn Rs.1000 plus perks. Sara also felt a need to grow in her career. The big thing happening at the time was the introduction of computers in almost all the industries.

Software for specific applications emerged in various fields. For engineering drawing and drafting, Computer-Aided Design and Drafting (CADD for short) was getting popular fast. CADD software packages meant for PCB design entered the market. Sara had a growing urge to learn CADD and upgrade her skill to designing on a computer. A few institutions for teaching and providing certificates in CADD sprouted up in Chennai. But she could not afford to enrol at any institution. The fees for these courses were enormous. It looked like the courses were meant for students from affluent backgrounds.

Sara's father could not possibly help. He had not supported Sara financially once she had started working. He did not even enquire how she was managing with her meagre income; not that he could afford to ask. Even if he wished to, her mother would not allow him to help her. According to her mother, feeding, clothing and educating Sara till the diploma was a very big charitable act.

On a lazy Sunday, she was browsing the 'wanted' columns in the dailies. One particular advertisement caught her attention. It called for a PCB designer to design in 'Smart Work', a computer app for PCB design. The interview was a 'walk-in' scheduled for the next Sunday.

"Hey Hari. There is this walk-in interview I want to attend in Adyar. It's this coming Sunday. Can you take me there?" she asked Hari the next day.

"Yes, by all means. I will come to your hostel next Sunday. We will go to Adyar."

"Sorry to bother you like this Hari. Sunday is the only day you get some rest. I am spoiling that as well."

"Hey, not at all. Anything for you. Also, we can spend a lot of time together on Sunday. We can go to a restaurant after the interview. Ha! Think about that girl," he winked.

That poor thing had only one day to wash and iron his clothes for the next week. He used to get some extra sleep on Sundays to recharge himself before running like a machine the next week. She felt bad about robbing him of that luxury. It was all because of her inability to go to a new place on her own. She was very poor with directions. She would be lost in any new place and would not be able to make her way back.

Hari insisted that he would indeed love to be with her rather than stay at home. He promptly appeared on Sunday morning on her doorstep and escorted her to the interview. She wondered why the hell he always went out of his way to help her like this. She felt bad asking for so much but he assured her that he was glad to do it for her.

Mr. Muthu, who interviewed her in Beta Designs, owned the establishment. The company undertook PCB artwork design work for many R&D units.

Circuit diagrams were provided by the clients and Beta Designs designed PCB artwork for them and delivered the films for fabrication. First, they would provide the clients with a 'check plot' which was printed in a dot matrix printer on a A4 size paper. Different layers would be printed on separate sheets. After getting approval from the client, the artwork would be plotted on an A0 bed plotter in 2x.

From the artwork plot out, the films would be developed in 1x, the same way as from a manual artwork sheet. Beta Designs processed up to this film. Clients would take this film from them and give them to the PCB fabricators to get the boards done. The design was charged anywhere between 25 to 35 rupees per square inch depending upon the complexity of the board. Mr. Muthu gave her a circuit and asked to design it in Smart Work. Smart Work was the popular PCB design software at the time.

"Sir, I do not know Smart Work. But given a chance, I will surely learn it quickly. I've been doing manual design for eight months."

He gave her a look which said, 'Then, what are you doing here at this interview!' Nevertheless, he decided to check how good she was and gave her the manual artwork tools and materials and asked her to design the circuit. When she finished, he inspected the artwork with satisfaction written all over his face. He was so pleased with her work.

"Good! You are a good designer. I can teach you Smart Work in two days, it is a simple package. When can you join?"

"Sir, I need to submit my resignation to my current employer and finish off the pending designs before joining here."

"Okay. Join as soon as possible. I will pay you 750 a month to start with."

She was very happy. She was going to learn computer-aided design with a salary that was almost double the amount she was earning. And what's more, she was going to sit in an air-conditioned room and do her job! The office and more importantly, the toilet were very neat and clean. She felt relieved. Hari was very happy for her.

The next day, she gave her resignation to Mr. Raj. She told him that she would always be grateful to him for what he taught her. He wished that he could have retained her. But he could not afford to give her that much of a raise. The other staff members were all senior to her. He would be obliged to give all of them a raise. Moreover, this girl was smitten with 'CADD' and he did not own a computer. So he wished her well and let her join the new company from the first of next month.

Now, Sara had moved to another office while Chitra was still working there, entertaining her colleagues with her usual stories of interviews she attended on a weekly basis.

The new office and job were very comfortable and satisfying. However, there was one thing Hari and Sara missed dearly; their morning meetings at the beach. Both their careers seemed to pick up pace but they missed each other very much. They met on Sundays. Hari took a room in a men's hostel, now that he could afford the rent. He had half-a-day off on Saturdays so he would promptly be present at Sara's office on Saturday evenings. They would walk to a small restaurant nearby, the IIT mess as it was named by the patrons since it was run by a bunch of IIT students in the evenings. Their *bajji, bonda* and samosa were very popular. Sara and Hari became regulars at the restaurant. Sometimes, they went to the nearby Besant Nagar beach before going back to their nests.

Hari had to manage his meals from low-cost outlets near his hostel. Most of the time, he lived on just bread and butter. He was already very thin and had a dark skin tone. This lack of nourishment rendered him thinner and darker. Only his eyes glowed with life.

Chapter 4

CLIMBING THE LADDER

Hari was earning a good name among his clients and his colleagues. Many colleagues befriended him; one of them was Alexander. Alex was in his late twenties, an MBA graduate who worked as an assistant manager in marketing in PC Link, a dealer for HCL desktop computers. His job involved selling PCs and software to offices and individuals.

Alex had a big dream; he wanted to establish his own business empire someday. He was already running a small business of his own, partnering with his school friend, while he had a decent ten-to-five job in PC Link. His own company, 'Joy Agencies' took painting contracts for apartment buildings. Apartments were the upcoming concept those days. His father had permitted him to use a tiny room of ten-feet-by-ten-feet for his office on the terrace of their house.

Alex's partner, Ramu was not as bright as Alex but a hard-working and honest chap. He followed Alex's instructions to the T. Every morning, he would come to the office sharp at 9, offer flowers to the pictures of Gods – both Hindu and

Christian, light exactly four incense sticks, close his eyes for exactly five minutes and murmur a prayer. Then he would dial the intercom sharp at 9:15 to call Alexander and say, "Good morning, Alex".

Alex would come upstairs to the office, give him instructions for that day, then go down get on his bike and go to his office. Since Alex was on the marketing team at PC Link, he had to traverse the city on duty. Most days, he would go home in the afternoon for lunch, take a nap for an hour and then go back to his work.

Meanwhile, Ramu would meticulously carry out all of Alex's instructions, have his lunch with the painters on-site, collect payments, purchase materials, supervise the painters and come back to the office in the evening. Then he would wait for Alex to return, give him a report on the day, submit the accounts and balance money, before finally leaving the office for the day. This pair managed to have a successful and peaceful partnership since they complemented each other. Brains, intelligence and work were well shared between them, with both of them playing their roles contentedly.

On a Saturday, Sara found Hari and Alex waiting for her when she left her office for the day. "Alex wants to talk to us about something important," Hari was smiling in amusement and looked like he had struck gold. She looked at Alex puzzled.

"Let's go to a good restaurant," Alex suggested.

They went to a posh one in Adyar. Unlike the restaurants Hari and Sara frequented, it looked grander, there were table cloths, comfortable chairs, dim lights hanging over every table and nice vases with fresh flowers on the tables. There was a mild fragrance in the air. The place was relatively quiet as the patrons and waiters were almost whispering to each other. It was an entirely different world.

The waiter laid napkins, forks and knives with the utmost care. Then he placed clean, warm, bone china plates. They were presented with menu cards. Hari and Sara did not know what to order. They were baffled by the names and pictures of the dishes. Alex ordered some fancy item for all three of them. The food smelled and tasted wonderful. Taking cue from the ambience, they ate without making noise. They whispered to each other too.

"Do you want anything else, Sara?" Alex asked.

"Do they have tea?" Sara was not sure if they served it.

"Of course, they have tea," Alex ordered it and the tea came in beautiful porcelain cups and saucers. It was steaming hot. Sara could not drink that much hot tea right from the cup. She poured some tea into the saucer and started to sip it. Alex watched in disbelief; he almost jumped.

"Jesus Christ! Sara, what are you doing!" Alex almost spilled his tea, "we don't drink tea from the saucer!"

Sara quickly realized that pouring tea in the saucer and sipping it, while a common practice in Vellore, was a no-no in Chennai. Hari was totally embarrassed but Alex regained his cool quickly and started conversing normally to make them comfortable.

They left the restaurant and went to the beach. It was very pleasant with cool breeze. The three laughed and laughed over the incident. Sara re-enacted Alex's expression, "JESUS CHRIST! Sara! WHAT ARE YOU DOING!" and again they laughed until tears poured down their faces and their stomachs ached.

"Alex, tell Sara about your plan," Hari prompted him.

"Oh sure. Sara, how about you two working for me?" Alex asked.

"What? How?" Sara did not expect this. "What work can we possibly do in your office?"

"I have a PC in my office. I can arrange to get your PCB design software. Using that set-up and your skillset, we can start a PCB design job work unit. I have even selected the name for the company. Joy Electronics," he beamed. "I would like Hari to resign from PC Link and join Joy Electronics. I can fetch computer service work from my contacts. I am also planning to take a dealership for HCL computers. I need a hardware engineer to install and troubleshoot PCs."

The idea of Sara and Hari working in the same office sounded good to them. Now, Sara understood the reason for Hari's excitement.

"You have a good reputation with your clients. You can easily get them to divert their design orders to us. I can bring in more orders since I am in the marketing field," Alex continued. "And I offer you both 2000 rupees per month."

The offer was just perfect — double their current salary and the chance to work in the same office which meant spending more time, almost all their time together. Sara happily agreed to the proposal.

It was agreed that they would get the artwork plotting and film processing done outside. Sara and Hari knew people at some of these facilities, so it could be managed easily until they bought their own plotter and set up a film processing unit.

Alex also suggested that Sara move to a better working women's hostel near his house-cum-office. She could afford a decent hostel now. Joy Electronics could be run in the same office where Joy Agencies was housed; on the topmost floor of Alex's house. Not his house but his father's. He paid his father rent.

With the extra income, Sara and Hari would be able to buy some good clothes and footwear. Hari would be able to afford better food. He could get some nourishment which was overdue. Poor Hari, being the ardent foodie he was, he had not been able to afford decent food for the past two years. One of Hari's dreams was to stack sacks of basmati rice at home when he became rich.

Hari and Sara resigned their jobs and joined Joy Electronics. Alex had the letter heads and invoices printed for the new concern. He also had business cards printed for Hari and Sara.

'Hariharan, DEEE, Hardware Engineer'

and

'Sarayu, DEEE, Design Engineer'

Wow! That sounded big! They were on cloud nine. It felt as if they had just been made Directors at Infosys. Alex knew how to keep people in good humor.

Sara moved into the nearby hostel. Hari vacated his room and took a small house on rent near the office. It had a hall, a kitchen, and a bedroom. His brothers started to stay with him on-and-off for their academics and job in Chennai.

Life in Joy Electronics was fun and interesting. Sara walked to the office from her hostel. She would go back to the hostel for a hot lunch and a ten-minute nap before returning. The orders kept pouring in. She always had work to do and never had free time. Alex employed an office assistant for her and she enjoyed bossing him around. Hari too had a lot of calls for PC service and software installation. Alex managed to sell a few PCs a month.

Alex treated Ramu, Hari and Sara with restaurant visits once or twice a month. Alex provided Hari with a two-wheeler from the office fund.

Hari and Sara became friends with Alex's and Ramu's families. Alex bought clothes for all of them for Diwali. They were like a happy family; spending time together, going out after office hours and enjoying occasional trips to restaurant.

Life at Joy Electronics was quite joyful.

Alex was a very religious person. His day started with a visit to the local church. He seldom missed the early morning service at the church, not even when he had an occasional cold or fever. If he were to go out of station, he would first check if there was a church wherever he stayed. He wanted everyone associated with him to be spiritual and religious, irrespective of what religion it was. When he learned that Sara was an atheist, he was surprised and even pained.

"Don't you believe that there is god, and he is the reason for anything and everything that happens in this world?!"

"Well, if there is a god, why do all the bad things happen in this world? Why is there so much misery and poverty? Why people inflict pain on each other? Why are there so many of atrocities happening and he prefers to be a mute witness to all this?"

"You cannot question god's way. You are not smart enough to understand that; no one is. Maybe people are punished for the sins they committed."

"What possible sin could the babies in the orphanages have committed? Take my case for example, my parents have four children. But my mom has always treated me like a live-in servant while she treated my sister like a princess. What sin did I commit to undergo this kind of childhood at the hands of my own mother? I don't even know the reason for her hatred for me. Did I beg her or this so-called god to give birth to me?"

Now, the discussion 'if god exists or not' was turning into a session on recalling Sara's bitter childhood. Alex had already learned about her difficult childhood from Hari.

'How on earth can anyone think of harming this fragile girl, let alone her own mother!' thought Alex.

"Let me tell you one thing. Only when you have faith in god, you can be at peace with your past," he insisted. "Let us do an experiment with god. Just do what I say without asking any questions. If it helps you in anyway, continue doing it. If it does not, you may just stop it. If you have faith in me that I am your good friend and I wish you well; do it."

"What do you want me to do? What experiment?"

"For the next one month, you are going to go to a shrine of your choice; be it a temple, a church, a *darga*, the choice is yours. I won't say that it should be this or that god. Just pick any god of your choice. Visit the shrine every morning before coming to the office. If you think that it gives you any peace of mind, continue; if it does not, you need not continue. You are not going to lose anything by doing this. Let's see if you can benefit from it. For me, Jesus is the light of my soul. I surrendered myself to him. Joy or sorrow, I share it with him and I am always at peace, no matter what happens. You try this for my sake."

Sara thought for a minute and said, "Okay. I will do it just because you are asking me to do it. If it does not work, I will drop the project and you should not be upset then."

"I promise, I won't be upset. In fact, you will thank me. Hey, the most important part of the deal is that you should do it for a month, without a break. All you have to do is to make sure that you sincerely try to communicate with your god; even if you are not successful for the first few days."

"If I say I do something, I do it with 100 percent sincerity. You can trust me."

"Good luck, Sara."

For the next few days, Sara checked with some small and big temples near her office. She did not feel anything divine or interesting, let alone feeling connected. After four or five days, she found a small Pillayar temple a few streets away. There was a big *peepal* tree in the front and the sanctum sanctorum was situated at the back of the shrine. She liked the temple for its serene atmosphere. The priest there was sincere and less greedy than the priests in the other temples she visited over the past few days. So she decided to stick to this temple for her morning visits. She also thought that this Pillayar had a friendly and smiling face. She would go there every morning, stare at Pillayar's face for five to ten minutes and tried to have a mental chat with him. But Pillayar did not seem to have any inclination to befriend her for the first two weeks.

Slowly, she started feeling a connection with him, started sharing her thoughts to him and had the feeling that Pillayar was listening to her. Before she realized it, the mental conversations started extending beyond five minutes. After every visit, she felt as if the burden of whatever it was bothering her, had lifted from her shoulders. She did not realize that a month had already passed.

One day Alex told Sara, "Do you know that it has been two months since you started going to the temple?"

"Oh my god! Really! Time seems to fly!"

"So, when are you going to stop going to the temple?" he mocked her.

"Alex! I thank you from the bottom of my heart for the help. I feel connected to god now. I feel Pillayar will take care of me, whatever happens. It is not my job to worry about my life anymore. He is watching over me."

"Jesus Christ! Look at her! She has even started giving sermons!" he laughed merrily.

Hari chipped in, "Sara, I will also go with you from tomorrow. I will come with my bike, pick up you at the hostel and we will go to the temple together." Hari had neither been an atheist nor a firm believer. He accepted the god factor but never prayed or went to temples. Now, seeing Sara so happy and at peace, he wanted to have the experience too.

Pillayar had become their best friend over this period of time.

✦✦✦

Alex's parents started to look for a bride for him. He had four siblings. The two elder ones were already married. Now it was his turn. After him, the youngest brother was to be married off. Then the parents would have completed all their duties towards their children. They found him a match and one Sunday was fixed for the 'seeing the girl' ceremony.

In India, the bridegroom's family would visit the probable bride's family along with some common friends and relatives to check if the alliance would work out. The pairs looks, the financial statuses of both the families, how much jewellery the bride would wear on the day of wedding, how much money she brought with her, what saree and jewellery the bridegroom's side would present to the bride and more would be discussed and agreed upon before fixing the betrothal followed by the wedding. This is called 'arranged marriage' while a 'love marriage' is where the boy and girl get married after falling in love with each other.

These arranged marriages are arranged within one's own religion, caste, and region mostly. Alex's probable bride, Mary, was a beautiful catholic girl from an upper-middle class family, who had just finished a Bachelor's degree. Alex and Mary liked each other and the would-be parents-in-law liked the would-be son/daughter-in-law. The financial terms and conditions were all agreed upon happily by both sides. The wedding was fixed to be conducted on a Sunday three months later in a big church. Alex was on cloud nine; he was head over heels in love with his fiancée. He started meeting the girl every evening and missing the after-office-hour meetings with Ramu, Sara and Hari.

Alex bought expensive clothes for Ramu, Hari and Sara for his wedding. They had a big dinner on the lawns of

Hotel Palmgrove after the wedding. Then he and Mary were gone on their honeymoon for almost a month. The office functioned without a glitch in the absence of Alex and all its affairs were managed by Ramu, Hari and Sara.

After the honeymoon, Alex's office-business-personal life became very busy. He spent a good amount on his honeymoon; all from the office funds. Then there was also an increase in his home-front expenditure. Slowly, the payment due to the vendors started to build up. Salary disbursement to Hari and Sara became very irregular. Also, Alex could not bring in new buyers for the PCs because he did not have enough time to concentrate on the business.

Hari and Sara were hoping that this phase would pass quickly and in due time everything would be well-handled by Alex. But as time passed, the situation did not seem to improve.

Meanwhile Ramu's wedding was arranged by his parents. They found a girl from an affluent family who brought a lot of gold and money with her. The betrothal itself was as big as a wedding. Close to a hundred people attended the function. The bride's side planned a big fat wedding with about 600 guests. They announced that the bride would wear over half-a-kilo of gold for her wedding.

Chapter 5

FINDING LOVE

It was Sara's twenty-second birthday. That morning, she finished bathing and took out her new clothes to wear. It was a present from Alex and Mary. The previous day, they took her to a boutique shop and bought her this piece. It was one of the very few birthdays she got new clothes to wear. Her parents used to tell her that they always bought her a new outfit for every birthday until she was five, before her sister was born. After that, on one or two birthdays, some uncle or aunt bought her something if they happened to visit them at that time. Her mother used to cite financial problems at home as a reason for not buying her something when a random friend or relative questioned her. But the month in which her sister's birthday fell always seemed to be a month of surplus.

She was admiring herself in the mirror when her roommate came in and said, "Happy birthday, sweety. There is a middle-aged woman waiting in the reception; she's asking for you."

'Middle-aged woman? Who could it be? Is it mom? Am I going to get one more hug and kiss from her, as a birthday present? Is she missing me since I left Vellore? Is that why she came to Chennai to see me on my birthday?' she was filled with so many questions. She could hear her heart's 'lup-tups' as she walked out of the room and went to the reception hall.

There was no mother. Only a timid-looking middle-aged woman seated on the sofa. Sara was disappointed and confused.

The lady rose and asked in a mild voice, "Are you Sarayu?"

"Yes, madam." She did not remember meeting this lady before. The lady opened a stainless steel tiffin box and held it in front of Sara. There were some sweets in the box.

"Happy birthday."

'What?!' 'Who is this and how does she know that it is my birthday?'

"I am Ravi's mother."

'Which Ravi? This lady has gotten the wrong Sarayu, I am sure.'

"Don't you remember Ravi? Studied mechanical engineering in college with you.'

"Oh! Ravi!! Ravi's mother!!!"

The lady was slightly annoyed by the fact that Sara did not remember Ravi. 'Is she not supposed to remember him, even if she is not thinking of him always?'

"Please be seated, madam. How did you know that it is my birthday? How did you know that I am here? How sweet of you to come to see me on my birthday! Do you live in Chennai?"

"No. I work in Vellore. I took leave for a day from my work and came to see you."

None of this made any sense to Sara. "Oh my god! Why did you have to do that?"

"Ravi pestered me to. You know, my husband died when Ravi was fourteen. I got a job in his office after his death. His father was an officer when he died. I got a clerical job on compassionate grounds. Ravi is my first son. I have one younger boy who is in high school now," the lady went on non-stop.

Sara looked at her with a sense of pity. 'Why is she telling me all these things?'

Ravi's mom continued, "Ravi joined in Royal Enfield as an apprentice as soon as he got his diploma. Last month, they made his job permanent. He has applied for a part-time degree at Anna University. He will most probably get an admission."

"Good to hear that madam…"

"He told me everything about you. He asked me to go and see you. He asked me to tell you that he remembers your birthday and he always will. He asked me to ask you to wait until he finishes his degree and then marry him."

Sara burst into laughter. The lady's face darkened.

"I know that my son is being insane. I advised him against this insanity. But I can't help but heed his consistent requests. I gave up and decided to do this for his sake," she said apologetically with a shrunken face.

'Oh my god! Have I hurt the poor thing by laughing out loud?' Sara felt bad for her behavior. She pitied the single mother. She put her hand around the lady's shoulders.

"You know what, aunty? I envy Ravi for having such a nice mother."

"I will do anything for the happiness of my children. They are the only reason for my existence," tears started to roll down her cheeks.

Sara waited for two minutes, wiped her tears and spoke in the softest voice possible, "But aunty, please understand that I am not in a position to think of my marriage any sooner. I have decided that I will think of getting married only when I turn twenty-five. I am not going to fall for any boy nor get engaged before that. I have a lot to do in my career before marriage and children. Please look for a suitable bride for your son when he is ready. Let me assure you that that lucky girl is not me. I can never think of Ravi as my life partner. I have other plans for life."

Ravi's mother seemed relieved when she heard Sara's decision. Sara saw a glimpse of happiness in the lady's face.

She had done what had been requested of her by her nagging son. She also got the result she wished for. She was happy that Sara was not interested in Ravi.

"God bless you, my child! May you achieve whatever you want to achieve in your career. God bless you with a bright future."

She gave the box to Sara and left.

Hari came to pick her up to go to the temple. They performed a special pooja to Pillayar and then they started their day at the office.

"Sara, I will finish the service call before five O' clock. Then we will go to Saravana Bhavan for dinner and then to the beach," Hari told her before he left.

The phone rang.

"Hello, Joy Electronics."

"Hello Sara. This is Krishnan."

A mild current passed from head to toe; just for a second.

"Hello Krishnan. How are you?"

"Happy birthday, Sara."

"Thank you! Glad you remembered my birthday."

"How can someone not remember somebody whom he thinks of twenty-four/seven?"

Sara blushed and did not know how to react.

"Sara, I work in Chennai. I thought of calling you and telling you earlier, but I thought I have to wait until your birthday."

"Wow. That's great to hear. Where are you working? How long have you been in Chennai?"

"I am in the middle of my work. I would like to talk in detail about everything this evening. May I take you out to dinner?"

"I would love to but Hari and I have already planned to go out for dinner. Why don't you join us?"

"That will be fine. Where are you going to?"

"To Peter's road, Saravana Bhavan. By seven."

"Alright. I will meet you two there at seven."

"See you then."

"See you, Sarayu!" The way he pronounced 'Sarayu' gave her a pleasant tingling feeling. Again there were butterflies in her stomach!

Krishnan met them at the restaurant with a big bunch of roses. He looked more smart and confident than in college. He worked at a big company at the other end of the city. He was sure of getting a part-time degree admission at Anna University in a few months. He kept talking about his job, his salary and pursuing his degree.

After they finished dinner, Hari settled the bill. He shook hands with Krishnan and told him, "Thanks for joining us Krishnan. Sara and I have planned to go to the beach. We shall leave now."

"I would love to join you guys, if you don't mind," said Krishnan.

Sara looked at Hari. For a second, he did not seem to like the idea. Nevertheless he said, "That's a good idea. Please join us."

They went to Marina beach, played in the waves, ate *sundal* and cut mango, and sat there talking till nine O' clock. Sara and Hari recounted the days they met there under the scorching sun. Krishnan shared stories from his office. He shared about his dreams and plans for his future. They spoke about common friends from college.

When they parted, the butterflies were long gone.

Finding Love

Sara had to go to Erode, a faraway city, with her family to attend her cousin's wedding. This cousin was her father's elder sister's first son, who was seven-years older than her. The aunt had another son who was four years older than Sara.

Earlier, her aunt asked her father to get Sara married to her elder son. He had refused to do so, citing the age difference between Sara and him as a reason.

In India, marriage between the sons and daughters of brothers and sisters is a common practice among Hindus.

So, this aunt was mad at Sara's father. The angry aunt looked at Sara and her family and melted at once; she welcomed them wholeheartedly and showered her affection on them. After all, she had another son of the right age and she could still have her for a daughter-in-law. She mentioned this to her dad twice during the wedding.

Sara's father had a younger sister, and she too had two sons, and she too expected to have Sara's hand for one of her sons. She dropped hints to her father about this.

"I am constantly being pestered with enquiries about your marriage these days. Looks like I need to dispose you of soon," her dad joked.

"Marriage for me? No way. Forget it, Pa," she replied seriously.

"What forget it? You have to get married someday and start your own life, no?"

"No, Pa. I would like to remain single forever. I have to achieve something big in my life. I feel like I am not meant for marriage, children and that whole lot of nonsense."

That evening, after the wedding, her father started a totally new thread. "A gentleman from the bride's side was talking to me this morning. Looks like they like you very much. They are eager to have you married to their son. He is an engineering graduate and works in the Kalpakkam atomic power station. They say that they can get a good job for you too at the power station."

"Marriage? For me? Appa, I am just twenty-two. It is too early to think about marriage. Moreover, I am not interested in marriage."

"Okay. When are you planning on getting married?"

"I am not going to get married at all. I will be a single independent woman. I have a lot to achieve in my career. I have to do my degree. I am not going to get married now. No way!"

"See, you cannot stay single forever. You have to get married someday. If not for you, for your younger sister's sake. No one will marry her if her elder sister is not married. That's the way our society is."

"Okay. Let me think of marriage when I am twenty-five. Not now."

"See, these people are rich. The boy is handsome too. Just let them come for 'seeing the bride' and then you decide. They told me that you can continue studying after marriage and they will support you. What's preventing you from accepting this good an alliance?"

What was preventing her? She did not have the answer. She was confused.

"Let me be free for another three years. Then I will think of marriage, I promise."

"You cannot think from your point of view only. Think of me. I have not saved anything big for your and your sister's weddings. It was a struggle to make ends meet. Only now your brother and you have started earning. And you have not given me any money so far. Where will I get the money for your wedding? If you earn and give me, I will save it and use it for your wedding."

"Who asked you to get me married in the first place? What's the need to save for my wedding now?"

"See, both my sisters asked me to give you to any one of their sons. You may have a valid point in rejecting them since they are not very educated. Last month your mom's nephew visited us. You know that he is an electronics engineer like you. He told us that he has joined in a good company and it would take one or two years for him to stabilize and, earn a good position and salary. He asked us not to promise your hand to anyone else until he is ready for marriage."

'What are all these people doing? Have they been waiting for me to turn twenty-two?'

"And you know what? Every one of these people told me that they do not expect any gold or money from us. They just want you to come home. They are even ready for a simple wedding. If I lose such a chance now, I will look a fool. When you say 'okay' to marriage at twenty-five, things might be different. They would have chosen some other girl by then. I might end up spending a lot of money at the time. And one more thing, we cannot be sure of people coming forward with such generous proposals for your sister after five years. It would be wise for me to save whatever I have for her wedding. Why would I want to spend money on your wedding when so many good offers are coming?

Just because you do not see the importance of grabbing this opportunity to settle down, I cannot spend the money which I do not have now."

"There is a whole lot of commerce and economics involved in a marriage, not just two hearts. What a world we live in!" Sara wondered.

"That's the reality. As a wise father, I have to utilize the opportunity when suitors are lined up for you. I give you the freedom to choose any one of these boys. I won't force my selection on you, though I think that this Kalpakkam groom is the most prospective one. It is up to you to select your life partner but do it faster. I have asked this Kalpakkam gentleman for a month's time. Decide before that and let me know," and so her father passed his verdict.

"What nonsense, Pa! Just one month to decide whom I should spend my whole life with?" Sara fumed.

"Yes. Thanks for understanding that. You have a whole month to think and decide. In case you have fallen in love with any boy, let me know. I will consider that too. I have no objection. But I won't spend my money on the wedding. That's my only condition."

She was greatly confused. If she got married and moved to Kalpakkam or any other place, what would happen to her work? How could she continue to be close to Hari if she got married to someone? Is not seeing or talking to Hari possible?

Finding Love

Sara returned to Chennai in an agitated state of mind. When she reached her hostel, she was running a high temperature. She could not eat. Her body shivered. She threw up a few times. Her friends at the hostel enquired about her health, asked her to take care and left for their jobs. She could not get ready to go to the office. She was alone and felt miserable. She missed her father. He used to pamper his children whenever they fell sick. He would take them to the doctor on his bicycle or sometimes he would even carry them on his shoulders and walk to the clinic if they were too weak to sit in the cycle carrier. He would nurse them, feed them patiently and give nice head and leg massages. She just wanted to go home and be close to him. At the same time, she did not want to go home and she wanted to avoid this marriage talk.

She was too weak to walk to the reception hall and make a telephone call to Hari. She took some tablets from her medical supplies and slept. After an hour or so, she was woken up by the caretaker of the hostel. "Sara, your friend is waiting in the reception to see you," she said.

She walked to the reception slowly. She saw Hari when she entered the passage leading to the reception hall. He was standing there, perturbed, walking back and forth. "Hari," her voice cracked and sounded like it was coming out of a deep well. Her eyes became moist. Hari turned and looked at her and his eyes were watery too.

"I was worried since I you did not come to work or call," his lips were trembling as he spoke. "What happened? You look so sick," Hari put his hand on her forehead to check the temperature. Tears rolled down Sara's cheeks. She was overwhelmed by his soft, warm touch. He looked into her eyes and a tear rolled down his cheek as well.

"Go, get dressed. I will take you to the doctor," he told her. "I will go to the office, inform Ramu and come back." The care and affection shown by him made her feel better. She took a quick bath and was ready when he came back.

They went to a nearby doctor. It was just a common flu. The doctor asked her to take the day off. She was already feeling better. "You go to work, Hari. I will have lunch at the hostel and sleep for sometime. I will be alright in the evening. Come to the hostel at five-thirty. We will go out for dinner." Hari didn't have the heart to leave her but there was work to do. He left reluctantly.

By evening, Sara felt better. She and Hari went to a small restaurant by the beach. When Sara narrated the exchanges between her and her father, Hari's stomach churned. 'How can Sara get married to someone? What will happen to me if I am distanced from her? How can someone else be closer to her than me?' He felt as bad as a child who has to share his favorite toy with another kid. 'But how can I express this feeling to Sara? What will she think of me? It feels to me like I have to grab her and make her mine forever. But what if she thinks of me as a brother? What if she got offended if I expressed my love, in the sense "love"' for her?' Hari was perturbed.

The next day, Sara was back to normalcy and went to work. Mr. Kumar, one of their regular clients, came to the office with a new job to explain to her. Since he visited them often, he knew both of them well. He was a father figure to them. As he sat and explained the circuit to her, he noticed that something was amiss with her.

"Sara, what happened to your usual 'brimming-with-enthusiasm' laughter and talking? You are so silent today. Is something bothering you?" Mr. Kumar enquired.

"Nothing, sir. My father is planning to get me married off."

"Oh! It's natural for every responsible father. Just go ahead and get married. What's your problem with that?"

"No sir…I can't do that…He has no money saved for my wedding and right now I am of not much help to him financially."

"Money is his botheration. Why do you have to worry about that? Just say yes to marriage and get settled in life."

"I don't want to think of marriage at all, sir. I would like to remain a single woman forever."

"Sara, let me guess what's really bothering you. You are worried about Hari. Right? You cannot leave him and get married and settle elsewhere. That's your problem."

'Oh my god. Is he a mind reader?!'

"I will tell you a way out of your predicament. Do as I say."

"What, sir?"

"You and Hari start your own business. That is a good enough reason for you two to stay together. I am sure, all your PCB clients will divert their orders to you." he winked.

Mr. Kumar kept on talking about the advantages of starting a business of their own. He assured her that he would divert all his orders to her. In turn, he asked her to reduce the rate per square inch for him and treat him as a special client. He said that there were a lot of new projects in the pipeline.

It felt like a foggy screen was suddenly lifted; she could see a clearer picture of the future before her. 'How good it would be to be your own boss and also be with Hari forever! Kumar sir, thanks for the valuable suggestion!'

That evening, when Sara told Hari about Kumar's suggestion, he felt like someone had dived in and saved him when he was about to drown in misery. It felt as if the idea opened a door to a meaningful life. 'How good it would be to be your own boss and also be with Sara forever! Kumar sir, you are a demigod to me!'

Sara had to visit a PCB manufacturing plant in Coimbatore, a big industrial city 510 kilometers away from Chennai. As a PCB design engineer, she wanted to know about the manufacturing process in detail. She had talked to the owner of the plant and he too had some jobs to give them. He asked her to visit the plant and take away the circuit with her. She had to travel to Coimbatore the following week.

Alexander was happy that Sara took the initiative of visiting the plant. "Can you go alone?" he asked in concern. Sara was famous for her topographical handicap. "Let Hari accompany you," he suggested. Sara and Hari happily agreed to the idea at once.

They took an overnight bus to Coimbatore. When they boarded the bus, it was almost full except for the last row. To travel in the last row of buses in those days was horrible. The nine-hour journey felt like corporal punishment. When they got down in Coimbatore the next day before dawn, Sara could not even stand straight. She felt like someone had dismantled the joints in her body and she trembled slightly. They took an auto to the factory.

When they reached the factory, it was six O' clock in the morning. The factory would open only at nine-thirty. But the owner of the plant was a kind person. He arranged for them to use the guest house of the factory until it was open.

"Get refreshed and have your breakfast outside. There are plenty of restaurants nearby. I will meet you at ten O' clock," he told them over the phone.

After stretching for a while and taking a hot shower, Sara felt better.

"The bathroom is free, you may go in," she told Hari. Hari went in to take a bath.

She got dressed. There was a small table on which a Pillayar was sitting. She folded her hands, said a small prayer and applied kumkum that was kept on the table on her forehead. She opened the windows to let some air in. The window opened to a beautiful garden outside. A cool breeze embraced her; it carried in the sweet fragrance of the flowers in the garden. She stood there mesmerized, unaware of time passing.

Suddenly, she felt Hari's hand on her shoulder. "Hey, what are you doing? Daydreaming?" he was amused as he looked at the transfixed Sara. He looked fresh, with a small streak of *viboothi* on his forehead. There was a twinkle in his eyes. Without even realizing what she was doing, Sara reached out with both her hands, put her hands behind his head, pulled his face towards her and kissed him on his lips. She released him, stepped aside and looked at him. Hot blood rushed to her cheek and she could not help but blush. Hari felt like he was hit by a mild electric shock. A pleasant surge passed through him from head to toe. The sight of a blushing Sara was amusing. He grabbed her shoulders and pulled her towards him, her face hit his chest and he felt like a big ball of snow hit him. He wrapped his arms around her and hugged her tight. Sara feared that a bone or two might break. It felt like a warm cloud enveloped her. He placed his chin on top of her head and the whole of her body stuck to his. Her cold body was slowly warmed by his warm body. She hugged him tighter and drew more heat. They stood there like that for a minute or two, which felt like an eternity and a fraction of a second at the same time.

When they parted, both of them felt an immense peace within them. Suddenly the future became very clear to the two of them. 'This is it. This is the person I want in my life. Together, we are going to flourish, become rich and raise a family.'

"Okay. Let's go out to have breakfast," Hari could not hide the joy in his voice, though he tried to sound normal. Sara tried to suppress her ecstasy but in vain; she was grinning from ear to ear.

They held hands as they walked out of the guest house. As they stepped out, they saw a small Pillayar temple across the road. It was just a two-foot-by-two-foot concrete structure with an iron grill. A priest was standing on the road in front of it and performing pooja. He prepared for the *harathi* as Sara and Hari went and stood in front of the temple. The priest performed the *harathi* then blessed them with the choicest of good wishes and gave them the offerings presented to the god.

The air was cool and it drizzled slightly like it was showering its blessings on them. They roamed aimlessly for some time before locating a restaurant for breakfast.

The owner of the PCB fabrication plant met them at ten as promised, took them around the plant and explained the process. Then he took them to his cabin and handed over some PCBs which were to be copied. In those days, copying an existing PCB and making slight changes to bring out another product was a very common practice. Sometimes, people just copied an existing design and used it for their products. PCB designers got such orders every now and then. They had to trace the circuit out of the existing board, draw the circuit and then a new PCB artwork, which should be an exact replica of the original one. This kind of job was charged double. Tracing out the circuit was a more difficult job than designing a PCB from a circuit diagram.

Chapter 6

THE BEGINNING OF AN ADVENTURE

Joy Electronics was well-established amidst clients when the new year — 1991 arrived. The days were hectic with lots of design orders pouring in. Sara worked for eight-to-nine hours a day, six days a week. Alex appointed an assistant designer for her. Hari had many service calls across the city and sometimes out of the city too.

But there was always a fund crunch in the business. Their salaries were paid in three to four instalments every month. For Sara, paying the hostel fee became more and more difficult every month. Hari was struggling to pay his rent as well. Something did not seem right. The PCB design orders kept coming as usual and the clients paid promptly too. All the money generated was draining into the paint business and for Alex's personal expenditure. They soon learned that Mary was in the family way. Hari and Sara suggested that Alex quit his day job and concentrate on the business full-time. But he had other concerns. What if he lost a well-paid job and the business failed too? He could not take the risk when he was going to be a father.

Sara and Hari kept discussing how to handle the situation. For Sara, there was another bigger problem. She was the one at the office all through the day. She had to attend all the phone calls. She found herself always answering to annoyed vendors regarding unpaid dues, giving some excuses as Alex had taught her and apologizing to them. This upset her day after day.

Hari and Sara felt that they had to have a serious talk with Alex and Ramu to end this misery. Another thought was also taking shape exponentially towards the end of April 1991. The seed sowed by Mr. Kumar had sprouted in both their minds. The thought, 'I don't belong to this working class where I go round and round with the same routine; I am meant for greater things' was branching out fast with each passing day.

On April 29th, Sara and Hari decided to talk to Alex the next day, to try and put an end to this uncertain phase of their life.

"The current situation has to change; it cannot continue like this forever," Sara said to Hari.

"Or, we have to do something about this. Even it means quitting Joy," Hari agreed.

"What if they get angry and ask us to get out immediately?"

"We have to take that risk. No point in prolonging this. If we have to leave immediately, so be it. We may find employment somewhere else. Or we may start on our own."

"Starting our own business! As of today, our savings are at zero."

"Let's take the risk. Otherwise, we will be stagnated here forever."

"Yes. That will be a more scary thing than being unemployed for a month or two.

April 30, 1991, Tuesday:

Sara had been working at double speed to finish pending orders. They needed to generate money for the first week expenses; rent, salaries and bills. After finishing a good deal of eight-hour non-stop work for the day, she stretched out, did some sit-ups, washed her face, had some tea and waited for Hari to come back from a service visit. Alex and Ramu entered the room.

"Sara, did you remind Mr. Kumar of the payment due? Tomorrow is the first of the month. We need to pay rent," Alex enquired.

"Yes. I did," she replied. 'I need to talk to Alex and Ramu now. Enough is enough.'

Hari entered the room, exhausted and sat down. Sara looked at him and asked permission with her eyes; he signalled for her to go ahead.

"Alex, me and Hari want to talk to you about something important," Sara said.

Alex and Ramu looked up from their desks. Sara's voice was strange. It did not sound like her usual assertive tone; it sounded rather meek. They looked at her inquisitively.

"It's very difficult to run life like this. Getting salary in three or four instalments, never having enough money in hand to spend," Sara looked at Alex.

"You know very well that things have not been going as planned for the past year. There Are outstanding dues from the construction industry. We are trying our best to collect the payments. Once I get the money, you will get your salary. But I still manage to give you the hostel fee and his rent every 5th promptly, no? Then what's the problem? Can't you take the balance in instalments?"

"Yes, we can. And that's what we have been doing all these months. But for how long is the question. What is your plan to rectify this situation? The money earned in PCB design is drained in other expenditures."

"Hold on. You cannot talk to me like this. It is none of your business to investigate from where the funds are coming and where they go. You are a PCB designer and please stick to that. Do you know how much I invested on this PC on which you are working? Do you know how much rent I am paying my father for this office space? There are many things that I manage here which I need not explain to you."

"Of course you need not explain it to me. But you are obliged to disburse the salary on the 5th of every month promptly."

"It's not possible given the situation right now. Do whatever you want."

"Okay. Hari and me are starting our own business. We quit."

Alex did not expect this. He was baffled.

"You will not get this month's salary," Alex declared. "Just get out of my office." Alex was as surprised as them by the words he uttered.

"Okay. Goodbye," Sara grabbed Hari's hand and they left Joy Electronics.

Thus, their two-year stint at Joy Electronics came to an end.

"Let me talk to the Auditor Balakrishnan tomorrow to discuss the possibility of starting our own business," Hari said to Sara as they walked to her hostel.

"Without any money, will we be able to start a business?" Sara was worried. "Just like we started Joy Electronics? Alex had already had an office space and the necessary infrastructure but we have to start from scratch."

All they needed was an office space and a PC. The price of a PC with a printer was around one lakh in 1991. Between them, they had around 800 rupees. They were not going to get April's salary, which meant they had to forgo four thousand rupees.

Hari put his arm around her shoulders like he always did when he wanted to express intimacy. "Sara, we have jumped into the ocean. If we do not swim, we are sure to drown. Let us try to swim and reach the shore. We have each other. That is more than enough."

'Yes. When Hari is with me, what is it that I am afraid of? What do we have to lose? Let us enjoy the adventure,' Sara's spirit lifted. She laughed merrily.

"Let's go meet Balakrishnan tomorrow. He will show us a way, for sure."

The Beginning of an Adventure

May 1, 1991, Wednesday:

They went to the Auditor's home. It was International Labor day; hence a holiday. Balakrishnan had an immense liking for the hard-working, intelligent and constantly cheery small town boy. They did PC service work for his firm. Hari always took good care of his systems.

The friendly Mrs. Balakrishnan brought out piping hot coffee. Their six-year-old daughter was playing with Sara while Hari briefed the Auditor about their quitting Joy Electronics and venturing into their own start-up.

After hearing Hari's account, Balakrishnan scribbled some figures on his writing pad, made some calculations and sat in deep thinking for some time. Then he said, "Go ahead, guys. You have a promising future ahead." He suggested that they take a PC on rent which would cost around 3000 rupees a month. And, there was the rent for an office which might be anywhere between 1000 and 3000 depending upon the location and size of the office. Would they be able to generate five to six thousand a month, was the question.

Mr. Kumar had earlier assured them that there were a lot of PCBs to be designed for his company as there were many projects lined up for the near future. The other clients would also give orders on a regular basis since Sara had earned a good name as an efficient and fast PCB designer.

"We will work on taking a loan sooner. My support and blessings are always with you," said the Auditor. He wished them good luck.

Hari and Sara were very hopeful of pulling this off quite well. Now, they had to name their business and come up with a logo. To Sara's designer mind, the logo had to be a graphic pattern using the initial letters of the name. The name should convey the line of business. It should be unique. No 'micro' in the name which was the trend in the '90s. She had been thinking very hard through the morning and none of the names occurred to her or which Hari suggested were good enough. If the name was good, she could not come up with a good logo for it. If she thought of good logos with PCB artwork patterns, names did not match with them.

They decided to perform a special pooja at their Pillayar temple that evening to mark the start-up. On the way they bought incense sticks, camphor chunks, coconut, bananas and some flowers to offer to Pillayar. As they entered the temple, a name and logo design came to Sara's mind in a flash. Circuits And Designs, CAD for short.

She immediately took out her scribbling pad and pen from her handbag, sat in front of Pillayar and wrote down the name Circuits And Designs, and below that drew a rough sketch of the logo. A semi-circle like a C in the left, to denote the first letter; a mirror image C in the right, to denote the last letter D; and an A without the middle line joining these two semi-circles.

Hari immediately approved of the name and logo. The name was catchy and the logo — awesome.

They went to the sanctum sanctorum to give the offerings to the priest.

"What is the special occasion today, kids?" the priest asked them as he came to them with a brass plate to receive their offerings to god.

"We are starting our own company, *Swamiji*," Sara replied as she put the offerings on the plate. And then she placed the piece of paper on which she scribbled the name and logo of Circuits And Designs on top of the offerings.

The surprised priest read the name on the paper, and said, "Circuits And Designs! Good name. May god bless you with a flourishing business." He performed their pooja with total dedication, gave them the *prasadham* (the offerings made to god, after the pooja is called *prasadham*) and blessed them profusely with a bright future.

Voila! They had just launched their start-up! They had become entrepreneurs!

They felt very peaceful and confident when they left the temple. On the way back Sara decided on the color scheme of the logo; sky blue for C and D and indigo for A.

Thus, Hari and Sara started their own business with a capital of minus four thousand rupees. This hard fact stared at them. What were they going to do? Now they had their personal as well as business overheads to meet. What was she going to do for the hostel fees and him for the house rent?

"Vacate the hostel and come stay with me. We can cut the hostel fees. I will ask for a loan from my parents. You can also borrow some money from your father, I guess," Hari suggested. Hari was the wiser of the two when it came to money. So it was decided that Hari would manage money and infrastructure, and Sara would take care of the design and customer care.

Sara started calling all her clients from public telephone booths and told them about their start-up. She would call the numbers in batches of two or three. Otherwise, she would earn the wrath of the people standing behind her in the line. Almost all the clients of Joy Electronics promised that they would give future orders to her. Now, the next requirement was a vehicle. They needed a vehicle to commute to clients' places and to the plotting and filming outsources.

Hari telephoned his parents and told them about the start-up and convinced them to part with 10,000 rupees. He went to his town on the 4th of May and brought the cash with him on the 5th so that he could pay his rent promptly. This was the first time that they held such a huge amount in their hands. This 10,000 would take care of them for the next three months. By then, they expected to receive some orders and payments from clients.

Sara called her father for help. He told her that he did not have any money to spare, but he offered to give his two-wheeler to them. It was a 100cc moped; a TVS XL. So their commuting was taken care of. Hari went to Vellore by bus and rode the 140 kilometer stretch to Chennai on the moped. He carried extra petrol in the side box of the moped.

Hari's house owner was initially hesitant to let Sara come and stay with him. But they convinced him that they were going to get married soon and got his permission.

They started hunting for an office space. The ones they liked were beyond their budget and the ones which were not very expensive were not very good. Finally, they had to settle for a not-so-good ten-by-ten foot room in an old building in a commercial hub in Nungambakkam. The advantage was that the office was located opposite a PCB fabricator they knew. People would find it easier to take the films from them and give it to the fabricator for processing. The rent was 500 and the security deposit, 2000; this was a concession rate because of the recommendation made by the fabricator.

With Hari's PC Link connections they got a desktop with a 286 processor and a dot matrix printer on a monthly rent of 3000. By the fourth week of May, 1991, they set up their office. Mr. Kumar gave their first order. As promised, he kept giving them many job orders and enjoyed a five percent discount. Sara started canvasing her old clients. Almost everyone diverted orders to them since they believed in the designer more than the concern she was working for.

Every morning they would wake up at six. Hari would cook their breakfast and lunch while Sara would sweep, mop and wash dishes. After packing their lunch, they would start by 9 O' clock, first to the temple and then to the office.

Sara used to sit at the office and design PCBs, while Hari went out for payment collection, to the bank and on some PC service calls. Both of them would go together to the clients' places for taking circuit diagrams and delivering check plots. After getting approval on the final design, Hari would go to the artwork plotting and filming vendors while Sara would start the next design.

Orders started pouring in. But still, every month, there used to be an anxious period, usually till the end of third week, until the bank balance equalled their overheads for the month — the rent for office, for the system, for the house, electricity bills, groceries, milk, and petrol. The last day of every month, they both sat down for their 'budgeting' for the next month. If the bank balance was greater by a few hundreds than the expenses of the next month, that was considered a good month.

Sara used to pray to Pillayar for a bank balance of three months' overheads. 'Oh god! Please bring us a period when we need not worry about the next three month's overheads,' was her usual prayer line.

God was obviously on their side because they never had a situation where they could not pay the rents or bills. Slowly the surplus in the current account started to grow to a few hundreds and then to a couple of thousands and then to a few thousands within a year.

Life was so sweet. At last, Sara got what she wanted. She was standing on her own legs with freedom from her mother.

But, strangely, she started having bad dreams in which her mother did despicable things to her. On stressful days, she was sure to have one of those nightmares.

The Beginning of an Adventure

Sara had a maternal uncle; her mother's brother. He was a branch manager at a nationalized bank. He was a member of the banks officers' association. He had many friends and connections within the bank as well as outside his work.

Sara suggested that they go and meet her uncle to find out the possibilities of getting a loan from his bank for buying their own PC and a printer. The rent for the PC, which was hired at 3000 per month was a major drain on their income. If they could get a loan, after four years they might have their own asset. It was some two years ago when she last met this uncle. She called him to find out if he could see them. Rajan uncle immediately agreed to see them.

Rajan uncle was a very friendly person. His very nature was to go out of his way to help those in need; friends, relatives, friends of friends or relatives. If someone asked for his help on something, they could consider it done. Rajan liked the two kids very much. He was amazed by the courage of these twenty-two-year-olds to launch their start-up with no money at all, to be precise, with minus four thousand rupees.

It was their good fortune that they contacted him and eventually became very close to him. With his help and guidance, they applied for a loan from his bank. He did not want to give them a loan from his branch since Sara was closely related to him. Instead, he made them apply to a branch near their office. Every rule relating to the loan was upheld, every procedure followed without any deviation, and all the conditions and terms applicable to any borrower were applied to their case. No rules were bent or circumvented.

They did not have anything to pledge to the bank as collateral security. Balakrishnan came to their rescue and he signed as one of the two sureties. Rajan signed for the second surety. Thus, after two to three months of running from pillar to post - application, approval, enquiry, rejecting, re-requesting, considering and sanctioning - they got their loan to purchase their own PC with a dot matrix printer.

This time, it was a 386 processor PC with an A4 size dot matrix printer. In 1992, upgrading from a 286 to a 386 was a quantum leap. It was another milestone in their life. Sara was so happy that her system and printer speed had increased.

They started receiving orders from the Wind Energy industry. A supplier to Vestas RRB was one of the major clients who gave orders worth tens of thousands. They could even hire an office boy to deliver check plots to the clients and for running other small errands.

Slowly, by the end of 1992, the bank balance reached a level to support the next six months' worth of overheads. They vacated the small office and their residence and shifted to a bigger house in Valasaravakkam. This house was newly built with good amenities and had an extra room that could be used as their office.

The Beginning of an Adventure

"Sarayu ma'am?" asked the visitor who was in his mid-thirties; he stood at the entrance. He read the name board once again to make sure that he was at the right address.

"Yes, sir. It's me." Sara smiled at him. "You must be Mr. Iqbal. I was the one who spoke to you on the phone yesterday, sir. Please come in."

He recognized her voice but was still not sure if this girl was the owner of the office. He was expecting to meet someone older.

She took him into the office room. "Please be seated, sir. Would you like some water, coffee, tea?"

"Thank you, I will take some water please." He looked around and was impressed by the office, run by a teenage-looking girl.

"Tell me sir, what is your requirement?"

"I am doing repair services to leather industry machines. Some control parts of the imported machinery cost a fortune. So I wonder if you can repair this PCB since you are into PCB design. I heard that your partner is doing computer services, will he be able to repair this faulty PCB?"

Sara went into the house and brought Hari to the office. Iqbal explained his requirement to Hari.

Hari took the board and inspected it. Then he said, "Sir, please leave the PCB with us for two days. I will try to solve the problem. What is this board used for?"

That was a PCB module used to control the automatic clicking machine in leather factories. The leather for shoe upper was placed over the cutting table and a heavy head with blades would come down on the leather to cut-out the shape of the shoe upper. That was the function of a clicking machine and this module controlled the automatic function of this process.

"What part of the process is not working, sir?"

"The power indicator is on. But the machine wouldn't move."

"Okay, sir. Give me two days' time. I will try to repair this."

Hari sat down to work immediately after Iqbal left. The voltage regulator was the culprit. It was burned and the power supply to the board was cut.

"I will go to Ritchie Street first thing tomorrow and the problem will be solved by afternoon," he grinned. He always loved this kind of work.

Ritchie Street is the electronics hub in Chennai; the one place for all electronic components and spare parts. The sellers there have connections world over. Even if a component is not available, they will be able to locate it from anywhere in the world and supply it. The boys working in the shops would not have finished schooling but the knowledge they possessed about the components was amazing.

The next morning Hari went there and bought a 7812 voltage regulator, a soldering iron, a multi-meter and a roll of soldering lead. He replaced the faulty regulator in a few minutes. Sara called Iqbal and asked him to come and collect the PCB.

"Oh! So soon! Thanks. What is the service charge?"

"Sir, I will check with Hari and call you back."

They were not sure if Iqbal would agree to pay 500 rupees for the job. But Hari incurred an expenditure of 400

The Beginning of an Adventure

for the purchases he made, including the multi-meter and the soldering iron.

"What if he does not agree to 500?" Sara asked.

"We can reduce it to 300. Anyway, the multi-meter and the soldering iron are going to be our assets. We can recover the cost over a few more jobs. If... we get more jobs that is..." Hari said.

Sara called Iqbal again. "Sir..., it...is...500 rupees."

Iqbal could not believe his luck. If he were to import the PCB, it would cost him around 7000 rupees.

"Oh well! I will take the board tomorrow, put it in the machine and test it, and I can pay you only after checking if it works."

"That's fine, sir. Please check if it works and then pay."

Hari and Sara did not know then that this would open a whole new avenue of opportunities for Circuits And Designs, and catapult them several steps ahead in learning and earning.

Soon they started having more than enough money in the bank. They bought good clothes and footwear. Hari bought his dream bike; a Hero Honda. Soon, their clients, vendors and friends started asking them when they were going to get married. They had been living together for almost two years at that point.

They had to wait for a few things before the wedding could materialize. One, Hari had an elder sister for whom his parents had been searching for an alliance. Her marriage had to happen before his. Another thing was that they had decided not to get any financial help from both families for the wedding. They decided to spend every paise required for the wedding from their earnings. Their parents were also not willing to spend on their wedding.

It was customary in Sara's community that the bride's father conducts and hence spends money on the wedding. While Sara's father was ready to solemnize their wedding, he was not ready to spend any money as he had declared two years prior. Even if he was ready to spend, Hari would not let him. He was man enough to earn and pay for his own wedding. Consequently, they needed time to save for their wedding.

Finally, by the company's second anniversary, they decided to get married. They needed a few months to make the arrangements and decided to have the wedding in November, 1993.

They sought the help of Rajan uncle to organize the event. He happily agreed to it. A good day and time was fixed for the wedding ceremony. Many of their friends pitched in to help with the ceremony, including their house-owners Mr. and Mrs. Bhashyam. They were very fond of the two of them.

The Beginning of an Adventure

'These two kids are not only earning their living at this tender age but also paying for their own marriage!' Mr. Bhashyam always had a soft corner for them. He was an admirer of their smartness and hard work. "Hey kids, is everything going as per plan? If you need any help let me know," he used to say.

"Sure uncle, we need your blessings mostly," Sara used to answer.

Sara and Hari bought silk sarees for Hari's mom and sister, and Sara's mom and sister. The sarees they bought to them and Sara were of the same quality and price. Sara did not even know about the 'bridal' saree collections. They went and bought six sarees; two of them meant for Sara — one for the wedding and the other for the reception. Such was their knowledge about dress material. Such was their knowledge about the way in which wedding arrangements were made. They also bought clothes for her father and brothers, his father and brothers, and for Rajan uncle.

When Sara showed the sarees and dress material they bought to the Bhashyams, they were quite surprised and annoyed by the fact that they did not buy a 'bridal' saree for Sara.

"Why did you not get a bridal saree? Why a normal saree?"

Sara blinked. She had no idea. "What is wrong with this saree, uncle?"

"You have got sarees worth Rs.1500 for your moms and sisters. Your saree is just Rs.1800. What kind of girl are you?" uncle chided in concern.

"Uncle, honestly, I have no idea. I never look at the monetary values of things. It's just that I liked those sarees and took them."

"You could have asked aunty before going. She would have guided you properly. We could have accompanied you," uncle said.

"We have a budget constraint as well uncle. We had only so much."

"You could have taken very good sarees for Rs.500 for the others. A good bridal saree is about Rs.5000. You could have spent the money on that."

"It's okay, uncle. This is the first silk material I am ever going to wear in my life. Unlike other girls, I never had a silk *pavadai*. That is why I am ignorant of such things. It does not matter what clothes and jewellery I wear for my wedding. What truly matters is the life after the wedding ceremony."

Uncle's and aunty's eyes grew moist. "This is the first time in my life I have met a girl who is smart enough to earn for her wedding and at the same time so innocent that she has no knowledge of sarees." Uncle and aunty and many other friends talked about her humble wedding saree for many years to come.

"Don't tell me that you are not buying jewels," Uncle cautioned. "A bride should wear new jewels on her wedding day."

"Oh okay, uncle. We will buy a simple necklace that weighs ten grams for me." She had never worn a chain before in her life. All she had was the small set of gold earrings that weighed two grams together.

The Beginning of an Adventure

"And you need to buy or make the *thaali* in gold," aunty reminded. A *mangalsutra* is called a '*thaali*' in Tamil.

"Every community has a different type of *thaali*. There are specific sizes, shapes and even weights. You should wear one which complies with Hari's family tradition. Ask your mother-in-law before buying one," Rajan uncle advised.

Sara called Hari's mom and asked her what kind of *thaali* they should buy.

"Are you kidding me? The mother of the bridegroom is the one who makes and presents the *thaali* to the bride. I have already given my ring to the goldsmith for making the *thaali*. I will fix a good day and time to start the process of making it. You don't have to buy any *thaali*."

"Oh! Amma, I did not know about these traditions. I am so happy that you are giving me the *thaali*. Please see that it is not heavy, I don't think I can wear anything heavy around my neck."

"It has to be exactly four grams according to our family tradition, I cannot do anything about it."

"Okay, Amma. Four grams is fine."

"One more thing, you have to wear the saree I give you when Hari ties the *thaali*. I have already bought you a silk saree."

Sara was overwhelmed by her would-be mom-in-law's gestures. God had sent her a good mother, at last. She resolved to be a worthy daughter forever.

Hari's father did not approve of their marriage. He would not attend the wedding. So, the wedding was solemnized by Hari's mom and Sara's parents.

Hari, Sara and Rajan uncle planned and executed every detail of the wedding ceremony within the budget. With the budget constraint they had, they could not afford the rent of a marriage hall. It was decided that the wedding would be conducted in a simple manner at a small temple; their favorite Pillayar temple in Valasaravakkam, followed by lunch at a small hotel nearby. Only close relatives and friends were invited to the wedding.

A week after the wedding, the reception was to be conducted in a bigger and better hotel where clients, vendors, friends and relatives could be invited. They preferred Hotel Palmgrove for the reception because that was where Alex's wedding reception took place. They could not think of any place more apt for the function.

The reception was fixed for the fifth of December. Hari and Sara went to Joy Electronics and invited Alex and Ramu to the reception. Alex was happy for them. He told them that Mary had gone to her mother's place for her delivery.

It rained heavily during the second and third week of November in 1991. Chennai was flooded extensively after many years of drought. Valasaravakkam was one among the worst-hit areas. Water, water, water everywhere. The whole of Valasaravakkam looked like a big lake on which houses floated.

Yet, all the people who were invited to the wedding arrived at the temple on the twenty-fourth of November.

"Rajan, you should have arranged for boat services to ferry us from the main road to this temple," was the joke almost everyone cracked upon arriving at the venue. The festivity and happiness was not dented in any way by

The Beginning of an Adventure

the flood. It was raining incessantly throughout the day, but the fun and frolic of a wedding was enhanced by the presence of their near and dear ones. Everyone was happy for them.

Sara wore the saree gifted to her by her mother-in-law; her new mom. The temple had arranged for a special pooja in honor of their wedding. The priest performed the pooja with added vigor. After that, the wedding priest performed the necessary rituals. Hari tied the *thaali*, which was handed to him by his mom, around Sara's neck.

Five minutes later, Sara got rid of her heavy headwear and flowers and tied her hair in her usual ponytail. The guests were all amused to see a bride in a ponytail.

After the lunch, their group, which consisted of the newlywed couple, Rajan uncle, Sara's parents, two brothers and a sister, Hari's mom, two brothers and a few college friends went to the Sub-Registrar's Office to get the marriage registered.

The Registrar was amused to see the bride in ponytail with just one thin chain around her neck. What was more interesting was the larger than usual crowd accompanying the couple.

The reception was held at the Hotel Palmgrove on the fifth of December, 1993.

The smallest hall was taken for the evening. She was in a sandal-colored saree with a maroon border. Almost all the guests at the event wore grander sarees and more jewellery than the bride. Nevertheless, she looked very beautiful. Hari was in a sandal-colored kurta with a maroon coat. They looked wonderful and happy.

Around 150 guests attended the reception party. Alex and Mary attended the reception with their baby boy. He informed them that Ramu had parted ways with him and started his own business of painting contract, funded by his rich father-in-law.

Hari and Sara never went for a honeymoon. For one thing, they had exhausted all their savings on the wedding. Another thing, they had job orders piling up during the wedding. The morning after the wedding, Sara started her sixteen-hours of work schedule, as Hari went on payment collection. The days following the wedding until the day of reception went by in the same manner. She worked extra-long hours to finish the pending orders before the wedding reception.

The days after the reception were also hectic and before they knew it, it was the end of December. Her twenty-fifth birthday came. Hari ordered a huge three-kilo cake from Bossoto Brothers. He got her a beautiful dress stitched from a popular dress designer. She was showered with chocolates, flowers and gifts. She was overwhelmed by the number of delicacies he cooked. They went to a fine-dining restaurant with friends and relatives for dinner. This was the first one of many extravagant birthdays she had later in her life. She would never forget that birthday though.

Hari had invited his siblings and Sara's siblings and father to the party. She cut the cake and took a piece to give to Hari. His brother was ready with a camera to click a picture. Suddenly, Hari lifted her and held her like a baby in his arms. That picture is a priced possession that decorates their living room.

That night, in bed, Hari said, "Madam, you are supposed to think of your marriage only this day onwards. But you are already Mrs. Hariharan now. What are you going to do now? Divorce me and look for a suitable groom?"

Sara laughed. "Did you ever think that the two of us would be married, say, three years back?"

"Yes. I did," he said.

"What?"

"I fell for you when we were in college but I never expressed my love to you."

"What! Why didn't you ever let me know about that? We were supposed to be best friends in college."

"That's why I did not tell you. I did not want to lose you by telling you this. You were rejecting every love interest and I was sure you would have done the same to me had I said 'I love you' to you. You were simply not interested in boys, I mean, not in the 'boy-girl' context."

"That is true…"

"Also, so many fair-skinned, good-looking boys were after you. I suspected that you would never consider a dark-skinned, small town boy like me."

"Stupid!"

"What stupid? Just imagine this. Had I confessed my love to you, you would have brushed me aside as 'one of those boys' overcome with infatuation. You would have cut the friendship totally."

'Hari is probably right. There was nothing wrong with some of the boys who approached me. Just because I believed I was too young and they were too young to fall in love and lose focus on their studies, I kept rejecting all of them. I could not stand such nonsense at that age. But look how things have happened! Even before I realized it, I am already married on my twenty-fifth birthday! Maybe this is true love and this is how it should happen!'

"What madam? Am I right or wrong?" Hari bantered.

"Of course you are right. But I am thinking of something else. Krishnan, Ravi and the other boys… I used to tell them that I would start thinking of my marriage only when I was twenty-five."

"So?"

"What will they think of me now? They would have been waiting anxiously for this day. What would have they thought when they received our wedding invitation last month? Wouldn't they have felt cheated? Won't they think that I bluffed them?" Sara's voice trembled. The thought of meeting Krishnan or Ravi ever again made her cringe.

"Hey, don't start now. I have been planning a super night today; a special birthday. Don't spoil my mood now." He pulled her close to him.

His moustache tickled her neck and made her forget Krishnan, Ravi, and the whole world.

Chapter 7

BECOMING SMARTER

The region comprising Ambur, Arcot and Ranipet near Vellore is the leather hub of Tamil Nadu. There are several big and small leather industries which have a major share of the leather export market in India. The leading brands from Europe and America got parts of their products like the upper section of a shoe, manufactured in India and exported back to them. They all had their cutting, processing and finishing machinery imported from countries like Italy. Our leather industry had a flourishing business in the '90s. Their machinery was at full throttle. When the parts went faulty, getting them repaired or replaced from their foreign vendors cost a lot of money and a loss of time. So, it was the practice of the plant managers to look for local engineers who could do the repair services and try to fix the problem with minimal cost and time.

This was the time when Hari was introduced to the leather industry. When it became impossible to take the control parts away from the machine to bring them to Hari, Mr. Iqbal took Hari with him to those factories. After a few of these visits with Mr. Iqbal, Hari started getting direct calls from the plant managers. Obviously, the plant managers wanted to cut the middle-man's cost by directly employing Hari for his services. It was a vast industry and many freelance electronics engineers like Hari found their green pastures there. Since they saved machinery worth lakhs, their bills for a few thousands got passed without any problem and the payments were also prompt.

So, to thrive among the competitors, one needed to have special skills to get more orders than other engineers. Hari traveled to those towns frequently on his Hero Honda bike, thereby cutting the lead time to attend to the problem quickly. If a call was made to Hari, the managers could rest assured that he would be present at the plant the next day. Most of the time, unlike other service personnel he repaired the machinery then and there. He used to carry the spares of the modules which are prone to fail due to electric spikes and overheating of machinery. Since he was able to shorten the lay-down period of the machine by reviving them on his first visit itself, he became quite popular in the industry. Also, his down-to-earth approach, cheery attitude and adaptability to the conditions of the plant made the plant managers chose him over other engineers.

Orders poured in, they shifted their office-cum-residence to a more spacious and good-looking building owned by the Bhashyams. Their outfits and accessories were upgraded. They both put on weight and their faces glowed. The income from the leather industry was one of the major contributors to cover their wedding expenses.

A couple of months after their wedding, they got a service call from Ambur. Four new machines developed the same problem at the same time. The machines were performing every other function except one particular movement.

Hari could not repair them on the spot. He brought back the control modules to Chennai. One particular component, a TRIAC was burned in all the four units. He got the TRIAC from Ritchie Street. He got the boards ready on a Saturday. He could fix the units on Monday morning if he stayed in Vellore on Sunday.

Hari used to halt at Vellore for the night and play cricket with Srini whenever he traveled to Ambur. This time, Sara also went to Vellore with him to spend that Sunday with her family.

Her mother would never welcome them whenever they went to Vellore. She would just give them a glance and disappear inside. Her father would come running out like a child, snatch their bags from them with a loud, "Come, come, come, Hari, come Sara," to make up for his better half's bad behavior. Her mom was not like that to everyone. This special treatment was reserved for Sara; not Hari. But now, since Hari was married to her, it was extended to him too.

Her father and Srini were eagerly awaiting their arrival. There was a special reason other than playing cricket. Dad told them that the three vacant plots adjacent to the house were coming up for sale. All the three plots belonged to one of his colleagues. She was quoting 12,000 rupees per plot. If someone could buy all the three plots together, she was ready to sell it at 10,000 rupees per plot.

Since Srini had been working as a teacher for two years and had some money saved, Father decided to buy one of the plots for Srini. He asked Hari and Sara if they could afford to buy the other two plots. He said that if they could, together they would be able to save 6,000 rupees.

Hari and Sara had never ever considered buying an asset like a plot. But when Sara's father asked them to think about it, both of them thought, 'Why not? Looks like a good idea! Owning a piece of land! For just 10,000 rupees! Seems quite possible…'

But, where from are they going to get that 20,000? The bank balance as on that date was only 15,000 rupees, out of which 5,000 was to be set aside for the month's expenses like rent, etc. They had only 10,000 to spare. The seller would not agree to give the plot for 10,000 if they were bought separately. The deal was for all three plots together as a package. But the seller assured Sara's father them that she would wait a month if they promised to meet the terms of the deal before that.

On Monday, Hari went to Ambur to fix the machinery while Sara rested in Vellore. When he came back in the evening, he brought back a solution to overcome the money shortage. He decided to bill the factory for 10,000 rupees for the service done for the four machines. The charge was on the higher side for the job done, but the managers in the factory were so pleased that he made sure production continued without any further delay that they readily agreed to pay him when he quoted the service charge.

In a few weeks, they bought their first immovable asset. They got it registered in Hari's name. Now, they were the proud owners of a piece of land on Mother Earth! They could build a hut, a factory, a farmhouse, or whatever they wanted! It belongs to them! The feeling was amazing and their happiness was unmatched. They went on to purchase other bigger and more prestigious properties later in life.

But they never got that kind of innocent ecstasy again, even when they bought properties worth Crores of rupees.

Life was not rosy all the way; they had their share of thorns too. They learned many lessons the hard way.

A manager at a leather factory asked Hari if he could develop a copy of a control module for a clicking machine. He assured them that he would buy five to ten pieces. He told them that there would be more factories that would buy in similar quantities, since this module was the one which failed often.

They also knew that this module was the one they often got for servicing. So, they began to design and develop a control module for the clicking machine.

First, the circuit has to be traced out from the existing board; Sara could do it in a week. Next, they have to hunt for the components in the market; two to three weeks. For the components which are not available, the equivalent ones had to be identified and sourced; a few more weeks. Then the drawing of the new circuit with the available components and for their configurations; he could do it in one week. It would take one week to design a new PCB with exactly the same dimensions and connector locations of the existing board. Then they would give the artwork for fabrication; the PCBs will arrive in two weeks.

Here came the tricky part. They had to pay a minimum set up charge for the PCB fabrication, whether they wanted to take just three boards or 1,000 boards. But if they ordered 100 boards, the rate per square centimetre is three-fourth the price if they ordered fewer boards.

Sara wanted to go about the numbers cautiously. But Hari insisted that they go ahead and make 100 PCBs.

What if they got more orders immediately? They couldn't wait for two weeks each time for the PCB to come.

Moreover, he had to purchase components and keep them in stock. The components available today might not be available tomorrow in the market. It is such an unpredictable market. Some components could be bought in tens. But some of them had to be ordered in hundreds, otherwise you wouldn't get it. The control board consisted of around seventy components.

So, they decided to take the risk and ordered 100 PCBs and 100 sets of components.

After struggling hard for three months and spending over 12,000 rupees which was more than fifty percent of their savings, they got the boards and all the required components in hand. They assembled five sample boards and tested their functions.

An R&D job is not an easy one. You need a super brain, a strong will, a tremendous amount of patience and perseverance to make a circuit work the way you want it to work. There are innumerable unknown factors that could make a circuit not work. After assembling the module, you have to detect and eliminate hundreds of bugs one by one, the process is aptly named 'troubleshooting'. You need to keep track of the number of permutations and combinations for the inputs and outputs of the module.

Hari was an electronic wizard. He had everything it took to be a good R&D engineer. He finally made the board work on his table. Now he had to take it to the plant, put it in the machine and make it work. That was an entirely different task. The board should behave in the real environment in the same way it did on his work table. When he tested it in the factory, the machine started working but it would not sustain the subsequent strokes.

After a couple of week's brainstorming and back-breaking, he discovered the reason behind the module's failure. The connectors they bought were not gold-plated like they were in the original board. When he replaced the connectors with ones from the original module, the machine worked fine.

Then the connectors had to be given for gold-plating or he had to import the original connectors. To import components, you need to have an Import-Export License from the government. The process of applying for the license and getting it after so many procedures and spending so much time, will delay the process. They could not afford both. The buyer wouldn't be ready to wait that long a period and he could decide to import the module.

Hari sent the connectors for gold-plating, which made a big dent in their savings. Finally, the gold-plated connectors were assembled in the boards. Hari took the boards for testing. This time they worked perfectly at the factory. The plant manager was very happy. However, he informed him that he was not empowered to make any purchases; it was done by the purchase department at their head office in Chennai. He asked Hari to give a quotation to the Purchase Manager and get the purchase order from him.

The next day, Sara prepared a quotation for the module, at 5,000 rupees per piece, and printed on their letter head. They took the PCBs nicely packaged in bubblewrap and went to the leather factory's head office. The Purchase Manager was known to them, since he was the one approving their service bills too.

Hari was on cloud nine on the way to their office. They kept talking and laughing about how tensed they were for the past few months; how stressful the R&D work was; how rewarding it was at the end to have made the boards work.

Now, they were sure of their next course of action — developing indigenized control modules for imported machinery of any kind, to start with, in the leather industry. With the success of this clicking machine module as the proof, they could request more orders for new controls. When they became rich, Hari would have sacks of basmati rice stacked at home for daily consumption! All they had to do was sell these 100 boards as soon as possible. 100 by 5,000 is five lakh rupees! Minus their expenses of 20,000 this was four lakhs and eighty-thousand rupees! Even if they had to deduct the overheads for six months, the net profit was four lakhs! Way to go! They are on the way to becoming rich!!

The Purchase Manager welcomed them with a sweet smile, offered them coffee and enquired about their business and personal life. He was such a friendly gentleman! He was in no hurry to unwrap the sheet and see the boards. After fifteen minutes of light chatting like this, he said, "Let me see the quotation," and started to unwrap it.

Hari took the envelope from Sara and handed it to him respectfully. The Purchase Manager inspected the modules and placed them on the table, took the envelope, opened it, glanced through and exclaimed, "What! 5,000! For this board!" he looked like he had just heard a big joke.

Hari's and Sara's hearts skipped a beat. They exchanged a horrified look. For a few seconds, they did not know what to think of and how to respond.

Hari was the one who talked first. "Err…sir…that quotation is for two boards. We supply one extra board as a spare for every board you purchase…"

The manager looked like he was recovering from shock. "Okay. That means 2,500 per board. Mmmm...still too expensive. Let me think about it. I will send you a purchase order for a suitable price in a week. You have to go to Ambur and install it there for no extra charges, if I purchase the board. Most probably I will purchase only one board to start with. We will see about buying more in the future."

Their enthusiasm ebbed and they sat there speechless for some time. They looked like two goats about to be taken to a slaughterhouse. Their faces became red and both of them secretly feared that tears would roll down from their eyes any moment.

The manager stood up, "Anything else, Hari? Nice meeting you both. I will send the PO in a week. You have to install the units the day after receiving my PO. So be ready. After getting the report from my production team about the satisfactory installation, you will get your payment in thirty days."

"Okay, sir. Thank you," they managed to mutter before stumbling out of the room.

They did not speak to each other for a long time. Then they went into a restaurant and ordered coffee. While waiting for the coffee, Sara went over the conversation in her mind and suddenly burst into laughter. She laughed so hard that tears rolled down her face uncontrollably. "Sir... the quotation is for two boards, sir..." she imitated Hari between bouts of laughter.

Hari chuckled in embarrassment.

She continued, "We can buy basmati rice on the way back home, Hari...hahaha."

Now her laughter infected him. He laughed until his stomach started to ache.

That was one costly lesson they never forgot. After a week of anxious waiting and praying, they received the order for two modules for 5,000 rupees. After a month, they realized the payment. Out of 100 boards, they managed to sell twelve boards over a period of three years. But they never ever again made the mistake of producing anything before getting a confirmed PO. More importantly, Hari learned not to count his chickens before they hatched.

Later in their life, they learned many lessons the hard way. After every lesson, they developed a strategy to counter such a situation in the future. But every struggle was a new one; every wound was a new one; every time they bounced back; every new lesson made them wiser; every heartbreak made them stronger. Day by day they became more and more tactful handling clients, vendors and staff.

Wherever they went, people used to admire their hard work and commitment to their job, be it a PCB design, service or production. Usually, the managers or supervisors or heads of departments who dealt with them were in their mid-forties. These people would have probably seen their own kids in Sara and Hari. They were all encouraging and helped them with orders.

Sometimes, they also stumbled upon people who exploited their innocence and lack of experience.

Mr. Vijayan was an accomplished entrepreneur. He manufactured and supplied timers and controls to many industries. He gave them a lot of PCB design orders, many of which required copying from boards that already existed. That is, the new PCB artwork has to be an exact replica of the sample given. This is a more difficult task than producing a new design from the circuit diagram. Sara had to measure and place the components at exactly the same location, and draw the patterns.

There were about a ten designs she had done over two months for Vijayan. Every board passed in the first instance unlike with his ex-designer. This encouraged him to order for the totally required number of PCBs, breaking the custom of ordering for just three boards for R&D and then going ahead with the total number.

As luck would have it, Sara made a mistake in a design. Without checking, Vijayan went ahead and ordered twenty boards. But to his dismay, the sample board did not work. While debugging the PCB, he found the mistake in the design and gave Sara a earful. He accused her of causing him a loss of 5,000 rupees. He went on to tell her that he lost sleep for two nights and was under great stress to finish and deliver the products to his clients.

Sara felt very bad. How could she make such a mistake, and cause great grief and loss to a valuable client? Her reputation as a good designer was at stake. She condemned herself. How could she repair the loss?

She called Vijayan and told him that she would re-design the board free of charge; she would bear the cost of the films; and she would bear the set up charges for the fabrication of the new boards.

"Oh! No, Sara. Don't be bothered about going through the whole process again. The loss I incurred is 5,000 rupees. Just compensate it in cash and I will manage the new fabrication. Take your time and produce the new design. You need not undergo the pain of getting them fabricated, it is part of my job anyway," he told her. He appreciated her for her integrity.

In two days, Sara and Hari withdrew the cash and went to Vijayan's office and handed the money to him. He took the money, assured them of further orders in the future as usual and asked her to produce the re-design leisurely.

When they left his room and crossed their production hall, they noticed that the same boards which he claimed were wasted because of the faulty design, were fully assembled and mounted on the enclosures, all the twenty of them. The quality-check team was testing the boards.

Sara went to the QC engineer and asked him, "Hi, isn't this design faulty? Does the board work?"

"Yes, there was a bug in the design but it was a small fault. We have corrected it by cutting a couple of tracks and soldering a few wires and the boards are working fine," he said matter-of-factly. "We are delivering the units this evening."

They stood there in disbelief for some time, not sure of what to think and then left.

"You cannot confront a client. It's your fault that you jumped to make up for his loss. He did not ask for it; it's you who offered to compensate his loss. He used your innocence to his advantage," Hari said. Sara felt embarrassed and guilty for losing 5,000 rupees out of foolishness.

"It's okay, cheer up. We earned good money from him. Nothing wrong in giving him back some of it," he consoled her. That night, both her mom and Vijayan appeared in her dreams.

There were many similar incidents which taught them about people and their behavioral patterns. They became smarter with the passing of time, to a point where Sara earned a name as a tough negotiator among clients.

Chapter 8

SPANNING WINGS

PCB design orders were pouring in from many industries such as ATM suppliers and Wireless solution providers. Whenever there was an interaction regarding the circuits, clients understood that Hari and Sara were capable of things beyond PCB design. They started discussing their technical problems in detail with Hari. Hari's insights and information provided solutions at times, that they invited Hari over to their labs to show and discuss their products. Such interactions led to opportunities to develop and supply control units to those industries.

One of the earliest products they developed was an interface meant for programming the channels and frequencies of the radios using an application software installed in a PC. The client, Metha & Co. was a walkie-talkie dealer supplying the marine department. He could not get his radios programmed to the required frequencies. He had an application software in his computer which could program the radios but he could not connect the radios with his computers. He asked Hari to develop an interface between the radios and the PC.

Hari conceived a circuit for the interface; Sara designed the PCB. After getting the boards, the R&D was brainstorming and back-breaking work for days on end. It was at a point in time when the internet was newly introduced to India. Hari explored information on the internet day and night, got solutions, sourced components, made several modifications in the circuit, had Sara design many versions of the circuit, and finally the prototype worked the way the client wanted it to work.

This is the case of each and every circuit and every instrument they developed and manufactured in future. It takes a brainy, hard-working, tough, never-give-up, never-getting-tired-of-researching, and ever-hunting-for-knowledge electronics engineer like Hari to develop a system, or an instrument as it is called by the electronics industry, which delivers results.

After the successful prototype, comes the sales and other commercials of the unit.

So far, they raised service bills to the clients and they used to get payments after getting the tax deducted at source. Life was very simple.

But now, it was time to get their company registered. They needed to raise sales bills with applicable commercial taxes and file and return the taxes every month to the government. When they were initiating the company registration process, they learned that a big multi-crore company had just registered the same name as theirs — Circuits And Designs. They were very big and growing fast. So, Sara and Hari had no other option but to find another name for their business to get registered with the Commercial Taxes office.

This time Sara named the company Accessteq Systems.

The lesson learned from the clicking machine control module episode was etched in their brains. They presented a quotation, got the price fixed after rounds of negotiations, got a firm purchase order and a fifty percent advance before proceeding to produce the units after the successful working of prototype. They fabricated just the required number of PCBs, bought just the required quantity of components and produced just the required number of instruments.

Accessteq Systems delivered its first product to Metha & Co., wrapped in bubblewrap. The good-natured Mr. Metha laughed at the way they presented the units to him. He advised them that if they wanted to grow big, they needed to show some professionalism in the packaging too. He asked them to put the boards in proper enclosures with the required provisions for the external connectors and deliver them neatly.

Thus, their education about enclosures was initiated. They did not know how to procure the standard plastic or sheet metal boxes meant for electronic instruments. When they tried to get custom-made fabrication done, the vendors were too big for them to consider their order value. They undertook large quantity orders only. The ones available over the counter in the market were either too big for their unit or they did not have the required cut-outs for the connectors. If they found the ready-made industry standards boxes in the right size, they were too expensive that using them would consume the entire margin gained from the project.

They searched high-and-low in the market for boxes for a few days. No luck! The client was putting pressure on them for the delivery. They did not know what to do. Finally, they stumbled upon a wholesale supplier of fancy items and located a plastic box meant for packing fancy jewellery. The boxes were made of cheap plastic in a bright pink color. But this was the best they could get a hold of. At least, they were of the right size and making cut-outs in that flimsy plastic material with a hot soldering iron would be possible, they reasoned. They were desperate to finish the project and get the payment.

They bought some twenty boxes for the first delivery. After supplying these twenty boxes and getting the payment for that, they might be able to explore further and procure better quality boxes for further despatches.

This time, Mr. Metha laughed with tears rolling down his cheeks when he saw the pink boxes with crude holes burned in them with the soldering iron.

"Never mind, I can make decent boxes from my regular fabricator," he assured them. "But you have to reduce your price for delivering without box." He made a price cut for accepting the units without enclosures. Hari and Sara had no other option but to agree to the condition. They had to forgo a marginal amount from the profit. Or else, they would lose the entire investment.

They developed and produced so many instruments for various industries which adhered 100 percent to the industry standards in the future. But, whenever Sara sat down to design an enclosure, she would invariably think of the pink jewel box and laugh. The 'jewel box enclosure' became one of their unforgettable episodes in life.

✦ ✦ ✦

Friends and relatives started pestering them with 'it is time you became parents.' Sara kept telling people that they would save enough before giving birth to a child. She used to tell them that 'project child' could wait another three years. But the family elders admonished her for such an irresponsible thought. They warned her that a child would not happen just like that whenever they opted for it. It might be too late when she decided to have one, they cautioned her.

In fact, Sara got pregnant the very next month after their wedding. Since they had spent all the savings for the wedding and did not have enough even for a honeymoon, they aborted the pregnancy. They never told anyone about this.

The Bhashyams advised them to have a child without any further delay. If they had children too late, they would become very old before the children finished their education and settled their life. That situation could be a scary one both to the parents and the kids, they insisted. Sara realized that it would indeed be scary and decided to have a child at the earliest.

Thus, Hari and Sara initiated 'project child' immediately.

Sarayu was sleeping in the recliner, a lovely smile frozen on her face. She must have been dreaming about the baby, about yet another pink frock, yet another toy and yet another book she was planning to buy for the baby.

She heard a familiar voice coming from far away. The voice grew louder as its owner, her mother, came closer. A splash of cold water hit her face. Now the voice had grown to a deafening decibel level, hurling despicable abuses at her.

Sara's breathing became rapid. Her eyebrows furrowed. Lips quivered. She tried to scream but her vocal cords refused to cooperate. She tried to run away but not a muscle in her body would move. She was staring at the beautiful yet terrifying face in front of her. She could not bear the abuses that came streaming from those beautiful pink lips. She was transfixed and terrorized. She wished that the verbal abuses would stop. The top of her head was in splitting pain owing to a blow delivered by her mother's clinched fist. Tears were rolling down her cheeks uncontrollably. She started to sob.

Suddenly, the abuses stopped. Her mother raised her left leg to kick her in the stomach. "No…! My baby…!" she screamed as she placed her hands protectively over her belly.

"Sara! Wake up. What's the matter, girl?" her husband was patting her cheeks gently. She woke up and looked at him. He was leaning over her, wiping her tears gently. She was drenched thoroughly in sweat. Her body was trembling. He made her sit up, cuddled her gently in his arms and kissed softly on her forehead. His concerned voice and warm hug brought her to reality.

"Nothing. Just one of those nightmares." She gave him an assuring smile. "I am alright."

"Another nightmare! But, it's been so long, may be a year since you stopped having these nightmares. What's the matter now? Were you thinking of a past incidents? I have told you many times not to think of your mother," he reproached her.

She too wondered what brought back that particular nightmare. Then she realized that she had actually slept for half-an-hour at a stretch. She had hardly been able to sleep for ten minutes over the past few months. The baby had been very active ever since it first kicked. How did she sleep for so long? Oh god! Oh god!

"The baby is not moving!" she gasped. He panicked and called the obstetrician.

"Don't worry, dear. I was expecting the baby to arrive before you were full-term. Check-in at the hospital at the earliest. I will be there in twenty minutes. Do not panic. Everything will be fine. It's almost thirty-two weeks. I will ask the hospital to prepare the theatre for a caesarean section," the motherly doctor assured.

'Hey honey! Want to see mom so soon? Hold on there, baby. Just a few more hours. You will see your mom and dad. Honey! You know what? Your mother is the best mother in the world. Yes, she will be the best mother in the world because she knows exactly how a mother should not be.' The baby gave a kick as if it understood.

"Come on Sara. Let's go. The cab is waiting outside." She checked the gas valve, switched off the lights and fans, said a quick prayer in front of Pillayar and they left the house. For Hari, everything happened in a blur – rushing to the hospital, letting Sara be wheeled into the operation theatre, signing the consent for a caesarean section, refusing the invitation to be present at the operation table and waiting outside for what felt like an eternity.

"It's a girl, Hari, congrats," the Doctor was beaming as she exited the theatre. "They are doing fine. Sara will come out of anaesthesia in an hour. Take care," she shook his hand and left.

A nurse carried the baby out to show him. Ananya had arrived! She looked like a bunch of roses. He held her in his arms. She was so tiny that she fit in a single palm. He could not control a flood of tears. The nurse stretched out her arms to take the baby back from him. "Its okay, sister. I know how to carry babies. I will take her to the room," he insisted.

"That's wonderful. Call me when they have wheeled the mother into the room," she left the baby with him.

He bent over and kissed her forehead. God! She is so soft and tender. His moustache must have pricked her. She let out a small whimper in annoyance.

He went to their room, handed over the baby to his mother who had come to the hospital to take care of Sara and the child, went down to the hospital's pharmacy, bought a razor, came back to the room, went into the bathroom and came out with his moustache shaved completely.

When he came out clean shaven, they were wheeling Sara in. She was still sleeping under the effect of spinal anaesthesia. His mother placed the baby by Sara's side.

He stood there and observed the fragile figures in the bed, lost in thought. 'I am responsible for two lives now. Oh god! We have not saved enough for the baby. We have to start earning multi-fold to give her a good life.'

Sara did not even know how to hold a new-born baby. The doctor had to teach her. She was surprised when she was told that the baby had to be fed once an hour. She had been under the impression that the baby would also feed three times a day, breakfast, lunch and supper, like any adult and go to sleep or play for the rest of the day.

God! It was only feeding and cleaning all the time for the first three months! What had she done to herself! But the little bundle of joy was worth it; worth all the suffering! They called her 'Honey' because she was their elixir, the source of their strength and motivation to work hard and earn more.

Ananya, their 'honey' grew up in the house-cum-office environment, playing with the PCBs, R&D table, tool kits and the computers. Her teachers were amazed by her technical vocabulary and knowledge in computers and electronic gadgets. Sara always heard from the teachers, neighbors and clients that Ananya was an intelligent and well-behaved kid.

Chapter 9

GETTING REWARDED

The next big step they took was in the direction of embedded systems.

They got two important opportunities to develop instruments. One to patch the land line phone with the walkie-talkie in moving trains and another from the ATM industry for a Video-Text inserter. Hari did not want to copy the circuits from the existing instruments. He wanted to develop their own instruments for those systems. There was only one way to do that; study and acquire knowledge about microcontrollers and learn to program them; in short, develop embedded systems.

An embedded system is a stand-alone computer designed to do a specific task. For example, an alarm panel installed in a bank triggers an alarm when a button is pressed by a bank employee; this is a simple stand-alone computer or an embedded system, designed to do that specific task under specific conditions.

Enquiries for developing such systems started coming in. And the urge to learn embedded hardware and software became greater day by day for Hari. But only the premier institutes taught that course and the fee they were asking for was beyond their capacity.

But if Hari wanted something, he would achieve it. He bought books on embedded software, pored over hundreds of pages on the internet, bought educational boards to do research, tried and failed hundreds of times before successfully teaching himself embedded system development.

Between his cooking, taking care of Sara and Ananya, playing cricket with the street kids, running to service jobs, he successfully became an embedded system developer.

All this was triggered by Ananya; her arrival into the world. Suddenly, he became a super responsible father. He needed to provide a good education, better shelter, fashionable clothes, their own house and a car for his princess. The little one had turned him into a responsible father.

All their sleepless nights, months on end of hard work had started to bear fruit. They started to get lucrative orders from prestigious clients.

EPILOGUE

The company grew bigger. They had around twenty-five employees. They used to work overtime most of the months in a year. They took buildings on rent to house the production, testing and packing units.

The phone patch for moving trains for Southern Railways; Video-Text-Inserter for the ATMs; access lock control for the ATM rooms; alarm panels for the banking industry; autodialers; energy-saving and remote monitoring for ATMs across the country; server room monitors for various industries; factory displays; LED sign boards for trains; and many small one-time process controls for various plants. These were some of the systems they developed and sold.

They bought a piece of land measuring 4,000 square feet in Chennai, built a three-storey, 6,000 square foot office-cum-residence building. They had their residence on the first floor of the building; administration was housed on the ground floor; R&D was on the second floor.

They bought many properties in the heart of the city. They bought expensive cars. Hari bought diamond jewels for Sara on her birthdays.

Ananya was sent to one of the best schools in the city. She shined in her academics and extra-curricular activities.

The couple who never had a honeymoon traveled to many exotic places across the world on vacations; they stayed on the 117th floor of the then-tallest building in the world - the 118-floor Ritz Carlton in Hong Kong; they had dinner on the Star cruise in Singapore on one of Sara's birthdays.

Both Hari and Sara did their part-time degrees in electronics and communication engineering from prestigious universities.

They plan for an early retirement, once Ananya finishes her studies and gets her post-graduation done in electrical and electronics engineering and takes over the company from them.

Thus, the humble and unexpected, rather unorthodox start of their journey into entrepreneurship took them places they would not have reached otherwise.

When you really want to achieve something in life, the entire universe conspires for you to get it, if you are deserving.

www.ingramcontent.com/pod-product-compliance
Lightning Source LLC
Chambersburg PA
CBHW020422220526
45464CB00002B/525